NATHALIE DUPREE COOKS
GREAT MEALS
FOR BUSY DAYS

ALSO BY NATHALIE DUPREE

Cooking of the South

New Southern Cooking

Nathalie Dupree's Matters of Taste

*Nathalie Dupree Cooks for
Family and Friends*

Nathalie Dupree's Southern Memories

NATHALIE DUPREE COOKS

GREAT MEALS FOR BUSY DAYS

Delicious Food and Easy Entertaining for a Less Than Perfect World

NATHALIE DUPREE

CLARKSON POTTER/PUBLISHERS
NEW YORK

TO RIC LANDS, BEVERLY MOLANDER,
MARGARET ANN SURBER, AND THE
TELEVISION CREW WHO HAVE HELPED
ME SO LOYALLY.

Published by Clarkson N. Potter Inc./Publishers, 201 East 50th Street, New York, New York 10022. Member of the Crown Publishing Group.

Random House, Inc. New York, Toronto, London, Sydney, Auckland

CLARKSON N. POTTER, POTTER, and colophon are trademarks of Clarkson N. Potter, Inc.

Manufactured in the United States of America

Design by Elizabeth Van Itallie

Library of Congress Cataloging-in-Publication Data
Dupree, Nathalie.
    Nathalie Dupree cooks great meals for busy days : delicious food and easy entertaining for a less than perfect world / Nathalie Dupree. —
        p.   cm.
    Includes bibliographical references and index.
    1. Entertaining.   2. Cookery.   I. Title.
TX731.D83   1994
642'4—dc20   93-40612
                                               CIP

ISBN 978-0-609-89960-1

146689836

ACKNOWLEDGMENTS

I must thank my editor, Pam Krauss, for all her help through the last book and this one. Her consistent guidance has been immeasurably beneficial.

The following individuals have influenced me in writing this book through their time, gifts, or inspirations—personal or printed: Rosemary Barron, Eileen Behan, Andrea Breault, Jane Brody, Kay Calvert, Judith Choate, Sam Collins, Will Deller, Crescent Dragonwagon, Alma Freedman, Joyce Goldstein, Jane Green, John Hadamuscin, Geri Hadda, Mimi Hails, Marcella Hazan, Nika Hazelton, Grandmother Kreiser, Raymond Kurzweil, Jim Landon, Richard Lands, Bob Lynn, Elliott Mackle, Abby Mandel, John Markham, Joan Nathan, Corrine Netzer, Marjorie Nunn, Molly O'Neill, Judith Olney, Ray Overton, Paul Prudhomme, Edward Safdie, Julie Sahni, Patti Scott, Margaret Ann Surber, Anne Tamsberg, Pierre-Henri Thiault, Lu Len Walker, Savannah Walker, Virginia Willis, Paula Wolfert, and Martin Yan.

I also need to thank my television crew that have stuck with me through the years: Anthony Marshall, Carlton Patterson, Clement McIntosh, Tom Loyd, Rudolph Ingram, Richard Perry, Vivian Baker, William Kimberly, and John Caldwell. They help make the food—and me—look good.

And a special thank you to Libby Kessman, who really kept the details straight while copyediting this book.

CONTENTS

INTRODUCTION

My home is the place where I am most myself. And, much as I enjoy the extensive traveling I do and all the grand restaurants I've eaten in during my lifetime, the essential me is a home cook. I am happiest in my own kitchen, with my cat, the constant chatter of birds outside, and my flowers, some of which bloom in Atlanta all year long. Sitting down to a meal I have prepared with good friends or loved ones expresses my feelings for them more clearly than any other gift I can offer.

I long ago decided I didn't want to be robbed of the joy of cooking for those I love, even though at times a relaxed meal with friends or family seems like a luxury. Life for me, while full and wonderful, is not perfect. My work includes an enormous amount of travel. The moments of glamour are intermixed with dishes and pots and pans, washing dozens of tea towels, ironing napkins, and planting pansies and begonias. And then there is the phone, and the letters from those who didn't get all the ingredients down after watching a TV show. If I don't plan ahead for family meals or special occasions, I simply can't do them justice. But with a little bit of forethought and by making the best possible use of my time, *whenever* I have time, I can feast family and friends with relative ease.

Perhaps one of the biggest kitchen myths is that hurried cooking, with the hysterical chopping of a whirling dervish cook preceding frenzied stir-frying or last-minute sautéing, fits best into a busy day. In fact, the opposite is true. Those recipes that could be started to cook and then left, either to cook on their own or to finish at another time, or those that can be precooked and reheated, served at room temperature, or frozen to defrost later, afford me the flexibility I need to fit gracious meals into a jammed schedule.

There have been numerous changes in my household (never a traditional one to begin with, as so few are today) over the last year, and these changes are nowhere more evident than in the way they have influenced my cooking. The two young women I think of as daughters because they came to live with me as teenagers have both recently married, and they and their husbands are frequent visitors in my home. Audrey, the elder, returned home for nearly a year while her husband finished graduate school, and when he joined her to job hunt, Pierre-Henri brought his Gallic tastes to the table as well. My parents, who are in their eighties, live nearby and we are in one another's homes regularly. My friends mean a lot to me, and I like to stay in contact with them. And I also have a roommate, who has her own life, but shares the kitchen.

Now that there were at least three of us who had to eat every night, I was back to thinking about "what's for dinner." Where a baked potato might have done for a solitary woman's dinner, it hardly suited a Frenchman. If anything boasted too much fat, Audrey uttered the damning words, "Too greasy." So I had to rethink some of my dinnertime standbys, lowering fat content by substituting yogurt cheese for cream cheese, boosting the flavor quotient with assertive seasonings, learning to rely more heavily on grains, salsas, and fresh vegetables and fruits. We all had different schedules, so the ability to reheat was crucial, as was the ability to prepare dishes in stages—marinating in the morning, for instance, and finishing off in the evening. God bless the microwave, not so much for cooking as for reheating.

Soups became more of a main course as well as a starter. After all, a soup is usually reheated easily, and we were able to incorporate leftovers as well. Breads, particularly homemade ones, have always been an important part of my diet. But this year we really got into making many-textured ones—full of grains, raisins and currants, and nuts, dark and rich as well as challah, light and cloudlike. One of my soups and one of my new breads are frequently enough for a meal.

At the same time, my staff was encouraging me to take a new, clear-eyed look at the recipes we were developing. Ray Overton, who has worked for me off and on for over five years, has a catering background and loves developing festive recipes that are conducive to good times with good friends. With his help, we applied the plan-ahead philosophy to dishes for entertaining. Margaret Ann Surber, whose association with me goes back nearly fifteen years, kept noticing the few pounds I had put back on in the last couple of years, and she, along with Kay Calvert, who provides clerical help, and Audrey, joined me in finding ways to excise fat from our recipes.

With their help and the experience of seemingly keeping several dozen balls in the air at all times, I have accumulated a bank of recipes that can accommodate all these different factors. The recipes in the pages that follow range from elegant appetizers and knockout desserts for formal occasions to simple hearty stews for family suppers. They are all designed to make the most of your time, however much or little you have to spare.

Notations on each indicate if a dish can be prepared ahead ⬤, if it can be frozen ⬤ or reheated ⬤, if it needs marination ⬤ (and a quick, last-minute grilling or sautéing), if it can be made earlier in the day and served at room temperature ⬤, or if it requires long, slow cooking ⬤. And many of these recipes can be prepared in stages. For example, you might brown the meat for a stew one day, then combine it with liquid and vegetables and bake the next; just be sure always to store any ingredients you have prepared in advance in the refrigerator, tightly covered. By matching the mode of preparation to the available time, you can design a menu that won't keep you in the kitchen slaving over a stove while your guests enjoy themselves. You can decide when you need to put in some kitchen time, whether in snatches throughout the day, or hours (even weeks) ahead.

A meal encompasses shopping and cleaning up as well as cooking. Grocery shopping is one of the biggest time eaters. A running grocery list means less wasted time in the store. Coupons clipped to your list speeds checkout. (I watch my favorite sleuth on Sunday nights and clip coupons then.) Shopping is faster at off-peak hours when lines are shorter and shelves better stocked. An extensive staple list eliminates the need to run to the store for just one thing. And precooked food in the refrigerator or freezer becomes like money in the bank.

Cooking is such a pleasure when I have time for it, when I start out with a clean kitchen, the music playing companionably, the phone silent, and I can anticipate having time to sit and enjoy the people I care for. When I am harried and pressured, when the laundry is mountainous and I have to mop up someone else's coffee spills, it can feel more like a chore. I must cook in snatches—marinating a piece of meat now, later browning it and putting it on to cook for a long time. In short, I can't afford *not* to plan ahead, and neither can you.

This way of cooking soon becomes second nature. I've learned never to do just one thing at a time in the kitchen. It's simple to put a chicken or a pot roast on to cook while the groceries are unloaded. Or pop a roast in the oven before the morning paper is retrieved; by the time I'm ready to leave the house, it's done. Many of these dishes, like Pierre-Henri's Lemon Chicken, can be left to simmer while I walk two miles, or write those letters, or call my parents, or pay bills. Then, when everyone finally arrives home, finishing touches are added, a salad tossed, and dinner is ready.

This is a book about the way we really eat and live today. I hope it will help you adopt a more relaxed attitude toward home cooking and make the moments you share with loved ones even more special.

Chilled Asparagus Soup with Shrimp ■ Cold Cucumber Soup ■ Carrot-Orange-Apricot Soup ■ Catfish Chowder ■ Smoky Eggplant Soup ■ Margaret Ann's "Better Than Chili" ■ Fennel and Bacon Soup ■ Mistaken Lamb Soup ■ Lemon-Zucchini Soup ■ Lentil Soup with Basil ■ Garlic Soup with Grapes and Croutons ■ Reuben Soup ■ Winter Squash Soup with Red Peppers and Mint ■ Sweet Potato-Apple Vichyssoise ■ Asparagus and Broccoli with Orange-Mustard Sauce ■ Oriental Ribbon Vegetable Salad ■ Garden Vegetable Salad

SOUPS & SALADS

■ Cherry Tomato-Jicama Salad ■ Spicy Asparagus Salad ■ Marinated Cucumbers and Red Onions ■ Fennel and Carrot Salad ■ Green Bean Salad ■ "A Different Kind of" Bean Salad ■ Fred Harvey's Coleslaw ■ Spicy Peanut-Cabbage Salad ■ Niçoise Potato Salad ■ Very Wild Rice Salad ■ Marjorie Nunn's Couscous Salad ■ Savannah Walker's Candied Apple Salad ■ Avocado-Orange Salad ■ Radicchio and Grapefruit Salad ■ Peach and Melon Medley ■ Citrus, Fennel, and Pepper Salad Topped with Feta

MORE AND MORE OFTEN, soup is lunch for me, along with a salad and some French bread. And on nights when we're all eating at different times a hearty pot of soup simmering on the stove and a sturdy salad that can stand in the refrigerator allows everyone to help themselves to a delicious, sustaining hot meal *whenever* they walk through the door.

Soup is the quintessential busy cook's dish. Once the ingredients are combined, most soups can be left to cook happily on their own, with a few minutes here or there not affecting the final outcome. They generally reheat with ease and freeze well, although some sensitive ingredients like eggs or cream should be added just before serving.

I long ago discarded the notion that salads can't be prepared ahead. Of course potato and bean salads and slaws hold well in the refrigerator, but to these traditional make-aheads add substantial salads of broccoli, fennel, or citrus. These salads are glorious creations, not just side dishes but culinary stars on their own.

Granted salads generally do require some labor-intensive cutting, peeling, and slicing, but they needn't be last-minute affairs. I clean my vegetables and salad ingredients when I bring them home. When I have a spare moment, I take them as far as I can in the time allowed— tear lettuce into large pieces, slice and seed peppers, peel and cut up carrots and celery, and refrigerate them all in airtight containers. Then I can feast on elegant composed salads (and better still, have quick, easily accessed, and nutritious nibbles!) all week long.

CHILLED ASPARAGUS SOUP
WITH SHRIMP

This soup is good hot or cold, and if I want a pretty starter, it adapts itself to the variables of spring and fall weather. It's a stunning green, so I usually serve it in flat bowls that have a contrasting pink, marblelike rim.

6 cups fresh or canned chicken broth or stock
1 pound medium shrimp
1/4 cup (1/2 stick) butter
1 onion, chopped
2 green onions, white part only, chopped
2 leeks, white part only, washed and
    chopped
1 carrot, peeled and thinly sliced
2 celery stalks, thinly sliced
3 pounds fresh asparagus, tough stems
    removed, and cut into 1-inch pieces

2 tablespoons fresh lemon juice
1 tablespoon chopped fresh dill
1 teaspoon chopped lemon balm
    (optional)
Salt
Freshly ground black pepper
2 cups half-and-half
GARNISH
Lemon slices
Dill sprigs
Sliced green onion tops

Bring the stock to the boil in a large pot. Add the unpeeled shrimp and cook until just pink, about 2 minutes. Reserving the stock in the pot, remove the shrimp with a slotted spoon, peel, devein, and set aside to cool. **This can be done a day in advance; refrigerate shrimp and stock separately.**

Meanwhile, heat the butter in a large skillet. Add the onion, chopped white parts of the green onions, leeks, carrot, and celery and cook over medium heat until soft and lightly browned, about 15 minutes. Add the cooked vegetables and the asparagus to the chicken stock and simmer 15 minutes.

Strain the soup into a bowl. Place the vegetables in a food processor. Puree until smooth, then add to the stock with the lemon juice, dill, lemon balm, and salt and pepper to taste. Refrigerate. **This can be prepared up to 3 days in advance.**

When ready to serve, stir in the half-and-half and adjust the seasonings. Add 6 shrimp to each serving and garnish with lemon slices, dill, and the green onion tops. Add any extra shrimp to the remaining soup.

Serves 4 to 6

COLD CUCUMBER SOUP

When it is too hot to heat up the kitchen or to move more than necessary, I am particularly grateful for this marvelously refreshing, simple soup. It's a wonderful starter before a tagine or couscous with chicken and
vegetables or a curry. It keeps several days in the refrigerator and because it
doubles easily I make a big batch.

4 cups plain regular or lowfat yogurt
1 cup fresh or canned chicken broth or
  stock
3 large cucumbers, peeled, seeded, and
  grated
2 tablespoons white wine vinegar
2 tablespoons olive oil
2 to 3 garlic cloves, peeled and finely
  chopped

3 to 4 tablespoons finely chopped fresh
  mint
1½ teaspoons sugar
Salt
Freshly ground black pepper

GARNISH
4 to 6 thin, pretty slices of cucumber
4 to 6 sprigs of mint

**CUCUMBERS
AND
BITTERNESS**
Taste cucumbers before
using them in any
recipe. If they are bit-
ter, sprinkle with salt
and leave in a colander
to drain for half an
hour. Rinse, dry, and
add as usual. This
process is a nice refine-
ment whenever you use
cucumbers but not cru-
cial if you are in a
hurry.

In a large mixing bowl, whisk together the yogurt and stock until smooth.
Stir in the cucumbers, vinegar, olive oil, garlic, mint, sugar, and salt and pepper to taste. Combine well and chill until ready to serve. Garnish each bowl
with a cucumber slice and a mint sprig.

Serves 4 to 6

CARROT-ORANGE-APRICOT SOUP

This delicate cold soup is a lovely starter for a warm weather meal, a picnic, or an outdoor concert. You may cook the onion, garlic, and carrots in the microwave to speed up the cooking and to reduce the heat in the kitchen. I usually prepare this in stages, cooking the onion, garlic, and carrots, finishing up with the broth a little later in the day, and then adding the cream just before serving.

2 to 3 tablespoons olive oil
1 medium onion, chopped
*2 garlic cloves, peeled and mashed to a
   paste with salt*
1 pound carrots, peeled and thinly sliced
1 teaspoon ground coriander
*1 cup fresh or canned chicken broth or
   stock*

1 cup fresh orange juice
1 cup finely chopped dried apricots
1 to 2 cups heavy (whipping) cream
Salt
Freshly ground black pepper

Heat the olive oil in a large, heavy soup pot. Add the onion, garlic, and carrots and cook over medium heat until soft, about 5 minutes. Stir in the ground coriander, chicken broth, orange juice, and apricots and bring to the boil. Reduce the heat to low, cover, and cook until the apricots are soft, 15 to 20 minutes. Strain the solids, reserving the liquid in a mixing bowl. Puree the solids in a blender or food processor until smooth, then stir back into the reserved cooking liquid. ***This can be done in advance and refrigerated or frozen***. Stir in 1 cup of the cream. Season to taste with salt and pepper. Refrigerate until well chilled. Add more cream to thin to the desired consistency. Serve cold.

Serves 4 to 6

CATFISH CHOWDER

The carrots add a lovely underlying sweetness to this soup, and the peppers really bring up the flavor of the fish. It's also very colorful. Catfish chowder doesn't freeze well, but it can be refrigerated for 2 or 3 days, it reheats well, and the flavors improve with time.

2 slices bacon, chopped
1 bell pepper, cut into ½-inch pieces
2 medium onions, chopped
2 large garlic cloves, peeled and finely
* chopped*
2 medium carrots, peeled and chopped
1 to 1¼ pounds boiling potatoes, peeled
* and cut into ½-inch pieces*
1 bay leaf

1 cup milk
2 tablespoons fresh lemon juice
1 cup bottled clam juice
1 to 1½ pounds fresh catfish fillets, cut
* into 1-inch pieces*
Salt
Freshly ground black pepper
2 tablespoons finely chopped fresh thyme
¼ cup finely chopped fresh parsley

In a large Dutch oven, fry the bacon until crisp. Remove the bacon and drain on paper towels. Pour off all but about 1 tablespoon of the fat and discard. In the remaining fat, cook the bell pepper and onion until almost soft, about 5 minutes. Add the chopped garlic and cook 1 to 2 minutes more. Add the carrots, potatoes, bay leaf, milk, lemon juice, clam juice, and reserved bacon. Bring to the boil, stirring occasionally. Reduce the heat and simmer until the potatoes and carrots are tender, about 20 to 25 minutes. *The soup can be made to this point and refrigerated a day in advance*. Add the fish, stir lightly, and cook until the fish is tender, about 5 minutes. Season to taste with salt, pepper, thyme, and parsley. Serve hot.

Serves 4 to 6

SMOKY EGGPLANT SOUP

MAXIMIZING YOUR GRILL
I love the smoky flavor of grilled vegetables, but sometimes I'm reluctant to fire up the grill for a small amount of food. However, when the coals are still hot after grilling meat or shish kebab I find I can use the residual heat from the coals to cook vegetables for the next day. Cut eggplants in half, brush with oil, and place on the grill, cut-side down. Grill whole peppers, turning once or twice to char evenly, and preserve in oil. Place thick slabs of onion on the grill to use in savory marmalades and grill thickly sliced potatoes for updated salads. Cook vegetables like zucchini, squash, scallions, and the like to top pizzas, sandwiches, or to use as a flavorful vegetable side dish—or a base for soup. Remove when done and use in a day or two.

I am in the habit of buying eggplant whenever I'm planning to grill something else, knowing that I can throw it on the grill while it's still hot from the previous dish. (See sidebar.) I can keep the cooked pulp for a day or so. This soup is one of the tastiest ways to use it, as the smoky taste really adds to the flavor. The eggplant can be cooked under the broiler but to get a truly smoky flavor, it should be grilled. You will taste the difference.

2 eggplants	2 tablespoons chopped fresh basil
3 tablespoons olive oil	1 tablespoon chopped fresh oregano
2 medium onions, sliced	Salt
4 garlic cloves, peeled and chopped	Freshly ground black pepper
2 tomatoes, chopped	Tabasco sauce
8 cups fresh or canned chicken broth or stock	½ cup freshly grated imported Parmesan cheese

Cut the eggplants in half and score the flesh. Brush the cut sides with 1 tablespoon of the olive oil, place on a hot grill or under the broiler, and cook until browned and soft, about 10 minutes. *This can be done several days in advance*. Scoop out the flesh and coarsely chop it. Set aside.

Heat the remaining olive oil in a large, heavy pot. Add the onions and garlic, and sauté over medium heat until golden, 7 or 8 minutes. Add the tomatoes and cook just until they begin to wilt and release their juices, about 5 minutes. Add the eggplant flesh and the chicken stock and bring to the boil. Reduce the heat to a simmer and cook 10 minutes. Add the basil and oregano and cook 2 minutes more. Strain the solids from the liquid, reserving the hot liquid in the pot. Puree the solids in a food processor or blender until smooth and creamy. *The soup can be refrigerated at this point for 4 to 5 days.* Return the puree to the pot and reheat to just below simmer. Season to taste with salt, pepper, and Tabasco and garnish with Parmesan cheese.

Serves 6 to 8

MARGARET ANN'S "BETTER THAN CHILI"

This nearly vegetarian chili is as filling as it is nutritious, and with the bulgur and black beans, along with a heady blend of spices, the meat is hardly missed at all. The flavors marry and develop the longer the chili sits, so make it at least a day before and refrigerate overnight. While it simmers on its own, I usually fix another quick meal for that night's supper. This freezes well up to 6 months.

2 tablespoons vegetable oil

2 medium onions, chopped

4 large carrots (about 3/4 pound), chopped

2 red bell peppers, seeded and chopped

2 green bell peppers, seeded and chopped

2 16-ounce cans black beans, drained and rinsed

1 cup bulgur, soaked for 20 to 30 minutes in 2 cups boiling water

2 16-ounce cans whole tomatoes and their juices

2 cups fresh or canned chicken stock or broth, or vegetable stock

1/4 cup chili powder

1 tablespoon ground cumin

1 tablespoon ground coriander

1/4 teaspoon cayenne pepper

Salt

Freshly ground black pepper

1 cup plain yogurt

6 green onions, sliced

1/4 pound Cheddar cheese, shredded

Heat the oil in a 6-quart Dutch oven. Add the onions, carrots, and the red and green bell peppers and cook over medium heat for 5 to 8 minutes. Add the black beans, bulgur, tomatoes, chicken stock, chili powder, cumin, coriander, and cayenne pepper. Bring to the boil, reduce the heat, and simmer for 30 to 45 minutes, until thickened. Season to taste with salt and pepper.

Serve in bowls with yogurt, green onions, and grated cheese as condiments for topping the chili.

Serves 8 to 10

FENNEL AND BACON SOUP

Now that we've cut back so much on bacon and sausage, using small amounts as flavoring in soups and salads is a special treat. These sinful little bits add an enormous amount of flavor to an already special soup. Perfumed with fennel, this hearty soup is a meal in itself and will keep up to 4 days in the refrigerator.

6 ounces bacon

2 large onions, finely chopped

2 garlic cloves, peeled and chopped

1 large fennel bulb, coarsely chopped

2 cups peeled and coarsely chopped potatoes

2 cups fresh or canned chicken stock or broth

3 tablespoons finely chopped fresh thyme

Salt

Freshly ground black pepper

In a large skillet or the microwave, fry the bacon until crisp. Transfer the bacon to paper towels, reserving the drippings. When cool, crumble into small pieces and set aside.

Add 3 tablespoons of the bacon drippings to a large saucepan or Dutch oven. Add the onions and garlic and cook until soft, 6 or 7 minutes. Add the fennel and cook for 10 minutes more. Add the potatoes and chicken stock and bring to the boil. Reduce the heat, cover, and simmer until the potatoes are done, about 15 to 20 minutes.

Remove the solids with a slotted spoon and puree them in a blender or food processor. The mixture should be smooth but still retain some texture. Return to the pan and season with thyme, salt, and pepper. Serve hot, topped with the crumbled bacon.

Serves 4 to 6

MISTAKEN LAMB SOUP

The next time you make leg of lamb, use the bone for this wonderful soup. This recipe was created by accident in the kitchen, but it was a very tasty mistake. Soaking the beans is not necessary.

1 leg of lamb bone	½ cup chopped fresh cilantro
2 cups dried navy beans	Dash of Tabasco sauce
12 cups water	Salt
1 large onion, finely chopped	Freshly ground black pepper

In a large stockpot, cook the leg of lamb bone, beans, water, and onion on medium-high heat. Let simmer for 3 to 4 hours. Just before serving, add the chopped cilantro and Tabasco and season to taste with salt and pepper.

Serves 8 to 10

LEMON–ZUCCHINI SOUP

When I met my first zucchini in London in the early 70s I never dreamed it could have so many uses—or so many companions, such as lemon. Combined, the two make a graceful, elegant soup. It can be refrigerated and freezes for up to 3 months.

2 tablespoons butter	1½ to 2 cups fresh or canned chicken
1 large onion, sliced	stock or broth
1 garlic clove, peeled and mashed to a	Grated peel (no white attached) of
paste with salt	1 lemon
4 to 5 medium-large zucchini (about	Juice of 2 lemons
2½ pounds), cut into ¼-inch-thick	Salt
slices	Freshly ground black pepper

In a large, heavy saucepan or Dutch oven, melt the butter over medium heat. Add the onion and garlic and cook until soft but not browned, about 6 minutes.

STOCKS
The best soups are those made with home-made stocks. Stocks are easily made from scratch, as once the meats, bones, and/or vegetables have been combined with water and brought to a low, steady simmer, they need absolutely no attention from the cook at all. I find the task of stockmaking is best done when I am unloading groceries and cleaning out the refrigerator to make space; any slightly wilted vegetables or leftover meat scraps can go right in the pot. After straining out the solids I chill the stock overnight, discard any solidified fat, and freeze in quart or pint containers.

Add the zucchini slices, cover, and cook until soft, about 10 to 15 minutes. Stir frequently to keep from browning and to ensure even cooking.

Puree the zucchini mixture in a food processor or food mill until very smooth. Return the mixture to the pan and add the chicken stock and lemon peel. Season to taste with lemon juice, salt, and pepper. Serve hot.

Serves 4

LENTIL SOUP WITH BASIL

This is a very hearty midwinter soup. If you omit the bacon, you have a virtually fat-free soup that is very high in protein. It freezes for 2 to 3 months.

2 cups dried red or green lentils
6 slices bacon
2 onions, chopped
3 garlic cloves, peeled and chopped
1 carrot, shredded
8 to 12 cups fresh or canned chicken
 broth or stock
2 tomatoes, seeded and cut into small
 cubes

1 10-ounce package frozen spinach,
 thawed and drained
3 tablespoons chopped fresh basil
Salt
Freshly ground black pepper
1/2 cup plain yogurt or sour cream
 (optional)

Pick over the lentils, discarding any small stones or debris.

In a large saucepan, fry the bacon until crisp. Remove the bacon and let drain on paper towels. Spoon out all but 2 tablespoons of the bacon fat from the skillet and add the onions, garlic, and carrot. Cook over medium heat until soft, about 5 minutes. Add 8 cups of the chicken stock and lentils and cook, covered, over medium heat until the lentils are soft, about 40 to 60 minutes, adding liquid if needed. Stir in the tomatoes, spinach, and bacon and cook until just heated through, about 5 minutes. Add the basil, and season to taste with salt and pepper. Serve garnished with a dollop of yogurt or sour cream, if desired.

Serves 8 to 10

GARLIC SOUP WITH GRAPES AND CROUTONS

This is one of those sterling recipes, simple but elegant. The garlic is full flavored but leaves no aftertaste, and the grapes add a subtle sweetness that contrasts nicely with the garlic flavor. For a chunkier soup, don't puree the leek mixture as finely. This can be made up to 3 days in advance.

2 tablespoons olive oil	Salt
1 cup chopped leeks, white part only	Freshly ground black pepper
12 garlic cloves, chopped	
4 cups fresh or canned chicken broth or	GARNISH
stock	6 slices bread, crust removed
2 tablespoons red wine vinegar	1 cup vegetable oil for frying
3 slices white bread, crust removed	4 ounces seedless white grapes, chopped
1 cup cream	

In a Dutch oven, heat the oil until hot. Add the leeks and garlic cloves and sauté until soft and translucent, about 10 minutes. Add the chicken stock and simmer for 20 minutes. Remove from the heat and stir in the red wine vinegar. **This can be done a day in advance and refrigerated.**

Meanwhile, soak the bread in the cream until all the liquid is absorbed. Transfer the soaked bread and the soup solids to a food processor or blender and puree until smooth. Add to the hot broth and blend gently. Season to taste with salt and pepper.

To make croutons: Heat the oil in a heavy skillet until very hot but not smoking. Cut each trimmed slice of bread into 9 cubes and fry until golden on both sides, about 1 to 2 minutes. Drain on paper towels. Top each bowl of soup with croutons and a spoonful of chopped grapes.

Serves 6

REUBEN SOUP

This is a hearty cold weather soup, perfect for a fireside supper or a Super Bowl party. With the garnishes, it tastes just like the traditional Reuben sandwich, sure to bring smiles of satisfaction from all who enjoy that hearty favorite. It freezes for 2 months. Refrigerate overnight to thaw.

1 3-pound corned beef brisket
2 cups sauerkraut, rinsed and drained
2 cups cabbage, thinly sliced
4 to 6 cups beef stock, plus ½ cup
¼ cup sherry or 1 12-ounce beer
1 onion, chopped
2 garlic cloves, peeled and chopped
2 tablespoons Dijon mustard
2 tablespoons butter
2 tablespoons all-purpose flour

2 tablespoons tomato paste
1 teaspoon salt, or to taste
1 teaspoon freshly ground black pepper,
  or to taste
2 teaspoons paprika
1 to 2 teaspoons caraway seeds
6 to 8 slices dark bread or pumpernickel,
  cubed and baked 8 to 10 minutes at
  350°F.
1 cup shredded Swiss cheese (optional)

Remove any fat from the brisket and cut the meat into 1-inch cubes. Set aside.

In a 5-quart stockpot, mix together the sauerkraut, cabbage, and 4 cups of the beef stock. Bring to the boil, then add the sherry or beer, onion, garlic, and mustard. Simmer for 15 to 20 minutes, adding up to 2 cups of additional stock as needed.

Meanwhile, in a small skillet, make a roux by melting the butter, stirring in the flour, and cooking over moderate heat until a light golden brown. Add the ½ cup of beef stock, tomato paste, salt, pepper, paprika, and caraway seeds. Stir and cook until thick and creamy, then stir into the hot soup. Add the cubed brisket and cook about 5 minutes, or until heated through. Serve in individual bowls garnished with the croutons and shredded Swiss cheese, if desired.

Serves 8

WINTER SQUASH SOUP WITH RED PEPPERS AND MINT

Winter squashes are not really winter vegetables at all, making their appearance in the garden well before frost and just as the green bell peppers have turned red on the vine. At this time the mint should be flush and full—a good companion for this soup. This soup reheats particularly well and can be frozen for 2 months; thaw overnight in the refrigerator.

STORING ROASTED BELL PEPPERS
Red bell peppers may be roasted ahead of time. Remove the charred skin and keep whole or cut into strips. I keep them in plastic bags or lightly covered with oil in an airtight container for several days.

2½ pounds winter squash (butternut, Perfection, Sugar pumpkin, or other), halved and seeded
1 tablespoon butter
1 tablespoon olive oil
1 large onion, finely chopped
1 garlic clove, peeled and chopped
1½ tablespoons chili powder
1 pound fresh or canned Italian tomatoes, peeled, seeded, and chopped, juice reserved

2 red bell peppers, roasted, peeled, and seeded, or 2 pimientos, cut into ½-inch squares
6 to 7 cups fresh or canned chicken stock or broth
Salt
Freshly ground black pepper

GARNISH
1 tablespoon chopped fresh parsley
1 tablespoon chopped fresh mint

Peel the squash, cut it into roughly ½-inch cubes, and set aside.

Heat the butter and oil in a soup pot; add the onion, garlic, and chili powder and cook over medium-low heat until the onion is soft, about 10 minutes. Stir in the tomatoes, and cook for 5 minutes. Add the cubed squash, roasted peppers, reserved tomato juice, and 6 cups of the stock. Simmer, uncovered, until the squash is tender, about 30 to 50 minutes. *The soup can be made to this point 2 to 3 days in advance and refrigerated.*

Thin with more stock if needed and season with salt and pepper. Serve the soup hot, garnished with the parsley and mint.

Serves 6 to 8

SWEET POTATO–APPLE VICHYSSOISE

NOTE: I make this soup in stages. I find it easier to put the potatoes in the oven and leave them than to monitor them in the microwave. While they are cooking, I have enough time to chop and cook the leeks and apples. If the potatoes are not ready, I still add the stock to the leek mixture and cook it. When the potato pulp is ready, I add it to the pureed mixture.

This soup has a tremendous amount of flavor with a silky smooth texture. It can also be served warm in the fall and winter. It freezes up to 3 months and will keep several days in the refrigerator.

3 pounds sweet potatoes (about 4)

2 tablespoons olive oil

1½ cups chopped leeks, white part only (about 4)

3 Granny Smith apples, peeled, cored, and cubed

6 cups fresh or canned chicken stock or broth

Salt

Freshly ground black pepper

1 cup heavy cream

1 tablespoon fresh thyme leaves

GARNISH

½ cup sour cream

Chopped fresh chives

Orange peel

Preheat the oven to 400° F.

Place the potatoes in the oven and bake 1 hour, or cook in the microwave according to your microwave directions, about 9 minutes on High. Let the potatoes cool to room temperature, halve them, and scoop out the pulp, discarding the skins. Set aside.

Meanwhile, heat the oil in a 5-quart stockpot. Add the leeks and apples and sauté over moderate heat until soft, about 10 minutes. Add the chicken stock and the potato pulp, bring to the boil, then reduce the heat and simmer 20 minutes. Remove the solids from the stock and puree until smooth. Add the puree back into the stock and season to taste with salt and pepper. *This can be done several days in advance.* Stir in the cream and thyme and refrigerate until cool.

Serve chilled or heat the soup almost to the boiling point and ladle into warm bowls. Place a dollop of sour cream in each bowl and garnish with the chives and orange peel.

Serves 6 to 8

ASPARAGUS AND BROCCOLI
WITH ORANGE–MUSTARD SAUCE

This is a wonderful spring–summertime salad that doubles or triples easily for a crowd. It can be served right away, with the warm sauce poured over the blanched vegetables, but it is really best when the flavors have had time to mingle and marry.

2 pounds asparagus, peeled, blanched 4
  minutes, and drained
2 cups broccoli florets, blanched 2 minutes and drained
1 red bell pepper, peeled, seeded, and
  thinly sliced
1 tablespoon sugar
2 tablespoons red wine vinegar
1 tablespoon cornstarch

½ cup beef stock
Grated peel (no white attached) and juice
  of 1 orange
3 tablespoons Dijon mustard
1 tablespoon mustard seeds
1 tablespoon Worcestershire sauce
Salt
Freshly ground black pepper

In a large bowl, toss together the asparagus, broccoli, and red pepper. Set aside.

In a skillet over medium heat, combine the sugar, red wine vinegar, cornstarch, beef stock, orange peel, orange juice, mustard seeds, and Worcestershire sauce. Season to taste with salt and pepper. Bring to the boil, reduce the heat, and simmer until thick and creamy, about 4 to 5 minutes. Pour over vegetables and refrigerate for 2 hours before serving. Serve chilled or at room temperature.

Serves 4 to 6

BROCCOLI
Broccoli keeps well in the refrigerator and can be quickly steamed or stir-fried for an easy green vegetable, added to soups and quiches, or pureed. I often cook a whole head even if I only need half because the extra keeps so well if it is just lightly blanched. To blanch broccoli, cut stem off, then peel and slice it. Separate the head into florets. Drop into a large pan of boiling salted water. Cook the sliced stems 5 minutes, the florets 2 to 3, after the pan returns to the boil. Drain and rinse with cold water, then drain again. Refrigerate until needed.

ORIENTAL RIBBON VEGETABLE SALAD

This is a simple salad I put together from leftovers found in the refriger-ator one day. Oriental sesame oil added tremendous flavor to a very unpretentious vinaigrette. Taste the dressing before adding more salt, as the soy sauce usually makes it unnecessary.

1 large zucchini, halved and cut into 3-inch matchsticks

1 red onion, halved and very thinly sliced

1 red bell pepper, seeded, halved, and very thinly sliced

6 green onions, thinly sliced

2 large carrots, peeled and cut into rib-bons with a vegetable peeler

1 8-ounce can sliced water chestnuts, drained

2 tablespoons sesame seeds

¼ cup sherry vinegar or rice wine vinegar

¼ cup soy sauce

1 teaspoon dark Oriental sesame oil

1 to 2 tablespoons sugar

Salt

Freshly ground black pepper

In a large bowl, combine the zucchini, red onion, red bell pepper, green onions, carrots, and water chestnuts. In another small bowl, whisk together the sesame seeds, sherry vinegar, soy sauce, sesame oil, sugar, and season to taste with salt and pepper. Pour over the vegetables and toss gently. Let veg-etables sit for at least 15 minutes and up to several hours before serving at room temperature.

Serves 6

GARDEN VEGETABLE SALAD

 hen the garden vegetables are just starting to peak, I can never limit myself to a single vegetable. I combine a bit of this and that to make a grand salad, the first promise of the bounty to come. Feel free to substitute any vegetables you have on hand. Add peas, capers, olives—whatever comes to mind. It keeps in the refrigerator for 3 to 5 days. I do not toss this in a bowl as the small bits will fall to the bottom.

3 garlic cloves, peeled and chopped
1 small red hot pepper, seeded and
  chopped
4 bell peppers (preferably a mix of green,
  red, or yellow), seeded and chopped
1 large red onion, chopped
1½ cups cooked string beans
1½ cups cooked butter beans

12 basil leaves, cut into strips
Salt
Freshly ground black pepper
1 small head red leaf or Bibb lettuce
2 tomatoes, peeled and cut into wedges
2 cups Basic Vinaigrette (page 149)
4 green onions, chopped

In a large bowl, combine the garlic, hot pepper, bell peppers, red onion, string beans, butter beans, and basil. Season to taste with salt and pepper. ***This can be done up to several days in advance and refrigerated***. Line a large platter with the lettuce. Toss the tomatoes and 1½ cups vinaigrette with the bean mixture. Pour the mixture over the lined platter. Garnish with the chopped green onions and pour the remaining vinaigrette over the salad just before serving. For a variation, use the Orange-Cumin Vinaigrette (page 150).

Serves 6 to 8

LEFTOVERS INTO SALADS
Some vegetables for salads do well cooked ahead, like asparagus, broccoli, and green beans, and I refrigerate or freeze them, ready for last-minute use or inclusion in my garden vegetable salads or Salade Niçoise. The longer they can be soaked in marinade the better, although green vegetables do discolor, alas. I reserve leftover vegetables like butter beans and string beans as well.

CHERRY TOMATO-
JICAMA SALAD

This very colorful salad looks and tastes best when you use red, ripe, and juicy cherry tomatoes. The jicama, pronounced "HEE-kah-mah," needs to be ripe, too. It looks like a chunky potato at a quick glance and is used so much in Mexican and southwestern cuisine that it has been called the Mexican potato. It is very crisp when raw and has a delicate, slightly sweet flavor. It's also good in stir-fries. If you desire individual servings, divide the ingredients among six salad plates, using the same layering procedure.

6 red leaf lettuce leaves

1 red onion, thinly sliced

3 cups halved cherry tomatoes

1 jicama, peeled and cut into matchstick
    strips

2 tablespoons chopped fresh cilantro

3 slices bacon, fried, drained on paper
    towels, and crumbled (optional)

2 garlic cloves, peeled and chopped

1 teaspoon mustard seeds

¼ cup red wine vinegar

½ cup olive oil

Grated peel (no white attached) and juice
    of 1 lime

Salt

Freshly ground black pepper

Sugar

Make a bed of red leaf lettuce on a large platter. Spread the sliced red onions over the lettuce. Mound the cherry tomato halves over the onions and sprinkle with the jicama strips. Top with the chopped cilantro and bacon, if desired. *The salad can be prepared to this point and refrigerated up to 2 hours.*

To make the vinaigrette, whisk together the garlic, mustard seeds, red wine vinegar, olive oil, and lime peel and juice, and season to taste with salt, pepper, and sugar if needed. Just before serving, pour over the salad and serve immediately.

Serves 6

SPICY ASPARAGUS SALAD

This dressing is so refreshing and full of subtle Chinese character that it goes with just about any dish. For a variation, use blanched green beans or Chinese yard beans.

3 green onions, chopped
3 tablespoons soy sauce
2 tablespoons rice wine vinegar
2 tablespoons Oriental sesame oil
1 tablespoon olive oil
4 garlic cloves, peeled and chopped

1 tablespoon sugar
½ teaspoon chili oil
½ teaspoon dried red pepper flakes
2 pounds asparagus, tips peeled and
   blanched

In a small bowl, combine the green onions, soy sauce, rice wine vinegar, sesame oil, olive oil, garlic, sugar, chili oil, and red pepper flakes. Mix thoroughly and pour over the cooked asparagus. Chill for at least 2 hours before serving.

Serves 4 to 6

MARINATED CUCUMBERS AND RED ONIONS

This salad can be made days in advance; the longer the vegetables stay in the brine the more "pickled" they will be. The brine will keep for at least a week, and you can add more vegetables (although the brine does get diluted by the cucumbers juices after a day or two).

3 English cucumbers, peeled if skins are
   waxed, and thinly sliced
Salt
6 tablespoons sugar
½ cup cider vinegar

1 medium red onion, sliced
2 green onions or scallions, chopped
3 tablespoons sesame seeds
Salt
Freshly ground black pepper

Sprinkle the cucumbers with salt, and let them stand in a colander for 15 to 30 minutes. Rinse and drain. Squeeze water out with your hands or a paper towel. Dissolve the sugar in the vinegar and pour over the cucumbers and red onion, green onions, and sesame seeds. Add salt and pepper to taste. Marinate at least 2 hours before serving.

Serves 8

FENNEL AND CARROT SALAD

This salad gets better the longer it sits, although we have never been able to keep it around for more than two days as it is so popular. It will add color and crunch to a special meal, and it can be doubled easily. This will keep in the refrigerator up to 5 days.

3 carrots, peeled and grated (about 2 cups)	*¼ cup olive oil*
	1 tablespoon finely chopped fresh dill
2 fennel bulbs, thinly sliced	*2 shallots, finely chopped*
6 slices bacon, cooked crisp and chopped	*1 to 1½ teaspoons sugar*
¼ cup red wine vinegar	*Salt*
1 tablespoon Dijon mustard	*Freshly ground black pepper*

In a large bowl, toss together the carrots, fennel, and bacon. In a small bowl, whisk together the red wine vinegar, mustard, olive oil, dill, shallots, and sugar. Season to taste with salt and pepper. Pour over the vegetables and let marinate at room temperature for at least 1 hour.

Serves 4 to 6

GREEN BEAN SALAD

 This is an amazingly good salad! I cook the beans ahead and refrigerate or freeze them. Defrost, if necessary, and toss in the salad. Of course, just-cooked beans can be used, too.

1 pound cooked green beans, or 2
*   10-ounce packages frozen*
12 to 15 cherry tomatoes, quartered,
*   or 1 15-ounce can tomato wedges*
2 tablespoons oil
3 tablespoons vinegar

¼ cup mayonnaise
Salt
Freshly ground black pepper
1 ounce blue cheese, crumbled
4 to 6 lettuce leaves

If using frozen beans, drop the beans in boiling water to cover. As soon as the water returns to the boil, drain the beans and refresh under cold water. Drain well. Place the beans and cherry tomatoes in a medium mixing bowl. **This can be done several days in advance and refrigerated.**

In a small bowl, whisk together the oil, vinegar, and mayonnaise. Season to taste with salt and pepper. Whisk in the blue cheese, pour over the beans and tomatoes, and toss well. Serve on a bed of lettuce.

Serves 4 to 6

"A DIFFERENT KIND OF" BEAN SALAD

Here is a very fresh-tasting combination of cherry tomatoes, green beans, and kidney beans. The mellow sweetness of the balsamic vinaigrette complements the subtle bite of the jalapeño, ginger, and dill.

2 cups green beans, tipped and tailed
2 cups halved or quartered cherry
  tomatoes
1 15-ounce can kidney beans, rinsed and
  drained
½ cup sliced black olives
1 jalapeño pepper, chopped
1 tablespoon chopped fresh ginger

¼ cup chopped fresh dill
2 teaspoons Dijon mustard
¼ cup balsamic vinegar
1 tablespoon olive oil
Salt
Freshly ground black pepper
Sugar

In a large pot of boiling salted water, blanch the beans for 8 minutes. Drain, refresh under cold water, and drain again. *The beans can be refrigerated for 2 or 3 days.*

In a large bowl, toss together the green beans, cherry tomatoes, kidney beans, black olives, jalapeño pepper, ginger, and dill. In a small bowl, whisk together the mustard, balsamic vinegar, and olive oil. Season to taste with salt, pepper, and sugar. Mix with the vegetables and let marinate in the refrigerator for at least 2 hours before serving. Toss gently just before serving.

Serves 4 to 6

FRED HARVEY'S COLESLAW

Historic restaurant recipes are a treasure trove for serious eaters and cooks. Travelers ate Fred Harvey's food aboard the Santa Fe Railroad's Super Chief, at the Grand Canyon's El Tovar Hotel, and in Harvey House restaurants across the West. Judy Garland played a waitress in MGM's 1946 hit film *The Harvey Girls*. The coleslaw can be made at a fuss-free time and stored in the refrigerator for several days. It isn't as sweet as it reads.

Modernized by my friend Elliott Mackle, this is as appropriate for a family-reunion picnic as for a slick foodie soiree.

1 head green cabbage	½ teaspoon salt
1 medium onion, peeled and trimmed	½ teaspoon dry mustard
1 carrot, peeled and trimmed	½ cup peanut oil
½ cup plus 1 teaspoon sugar	½ cup white vinegar
½ teaspoon celery seeds	

In a food processor or by hand, shred the cabbage, onion, and carrot. Place the vegetables in a glass bowl or crock with a tight-fitting lid. Sprinkle with ½ cup sugar and the celery seeds.

In a small saucepan, bring the salt, dry mustard, oil, vinegar, and 1 teaspoon sugar to the boil. Lower the heat and simmer for a minute or so, whisking occasionally. Remove from the heat and pour the dressing over the cabbage. Toss lightly and let stand, covered, for at least 4 hours, then refrigerate. Toss again before serving.

Serves 8

SPICY PEANUT–CABBAGE SALAD

When fall and winter come, it becomes increasingly difficult to make a pretty salad. This one is multicolored and multitextured, has a very interesting flavor, and has multiuses—as well as having an enormous amount of personality. Like many cold cabbage dishes, it is better made ahead.

Whether you serve it cold as an accompaniment to grilled pork, poultry, or lamb; as a leftover; or as a hot salad stir-fried just until the cabbage wilts, you'll like having this multifaceted salad around.

½ head red cabbage, cored and thinly
   sliced
½ head green cabbage, cored and thinly
   sliced
2 carrots, peeled and grated
1 red bell pepper, cut into julienne strips
2 garlic cloves, peeled and chopped
3 green onions, chopped
¼ cup coarsely chopped cilantro
1 hot pepper, chopped, or 1 teaspoon hot
   red pepper flakes
¼ cup chopped roasted unsalted peanuts
½ cup plain yogurt

3 tablespoons peanut butter
¼ cup red wine vinegar
3 tablespoons olive oil
2 teaspoons dark Oriental sesame oil
½ cup fresh or canned chicken stock or
   broth
Salt
Freshly ground black pepper
Sugar

GARNISH

¼ cup chopped peanuts
2 tablespoons chopped cilantro

In a large bowl, mix together the cabbages, carrots, and red bell pepper. In a separate bowl, combine the garlic, green onions, cilantro, hot pepper, peanuts, yogurt, peanut butter, red wine vinegar, olive oil, sesame oil, chicken stock, and salt, pepper, and sugar to taste. Whisk until thick and creamy.

Pour the dressing over the cabbage and toss well. Refrigerate for at least 2 hours. **The salad can be made to this point a day or 2 in advance.** Toss just before serving and sprinkle with additional chopped peanuts and cilantro.

Serves 6 to 8

NIÇOISE POTATO SALAD

My first Salade Niçoise was a revelation to me: Tiny French beans, half the width of my little finger, tossed with olives, anchovies, tomatoes, and tuna, served on the patio of my friend Chester's home in Cap d'Antibes, France, prepared by a dragon of a cook who answered no questions but cooked like an angel. Later, at the Cordon Bleu, I learned that olives, anchovies, and tuna are hallmarks of a Salade Niçoise, and technically, that a Salade Niçoise is equal amounts of diced potatoes and green beans in a vinaigrette with tomatoes and garnished with anchovies and olives. Frankly, I even think it's okay to omit the anchovies to please the Philistines in your family if you want a refreshing summer salad that can be made quickly and used as an appetizer or the whole meal. Needless to say, it's great for a picnic or boating.

2 pounds unpeeled small red new potatoes, cooked and cut into quarters
½ pound green beans, cooked tender-
  crisp and cut into 1-inch pieces
8 to 10 black olives, sliced
10 to 12 cherry tomatoes, halved
3 hard-cooked eggs, peeled and diced
¼ cup mayonnaise or yogurt
1 tablespoon Dijon mustard

2 tablespoons lemon juice
2 to 3 tablespoons finely chopped fresh
  parsley
3 to 4 anchovies, drained
1 6-ounce can tuna, drained, or equivalent amount of cooked and shredded
  fish
Salt
Freshly ground black pepper

In a large mixing bowl, toss together the potatoes, green beans, olives, cherry tomatoes, and eggs.

In a blender or food processor, combine the mayonnaise, mustard, lemon juice, parsley, anchovies, and tuna. Season to taste with salt and pepper. Process until smooth. Pour over the potato and green bean mixture and toss to coat well. *This can be done up to 3 hours in advance.* Chill until ready to serve.

Serves 4 to 6

VERY WILD RICE SALAD

STORING DRESSING

I no longer believe in the theory that dressings should be made at the last minute. I make them up in large batches and vary them by adding a little Oriental sesame oil, capers, olives, or ginger. Keep them in the refrigerator in jars with tight-fitting lids.

Bob Lynn, who develops recipes for the restaurant chain Houston's, drops by on occasion to share a recipe or to take a class. His recipes have never disappointed us. This one is fabulous, full of crunch and flavor. I love it with game—in fact, I love it anytime. Make sure the figs, celery, onion, and scallions are finely chopped into ⅛-inch × ⅛-inch pieces.

4 cups water or chicken stock
1 cup wild rice, rinsed thoroughly under
  running water

DRESSING
2 tablespoons raspberry or red wine
  vinegar
1 tablespoon lemon juice
1 garlic clove, peeled and finely chopped
1 teaspoon Dijon mustard
1 teaspoon sugar
1 teaspoon kosher salt
¼ teaspoon pepper

½ cup vegetable or peanut oil
¼ cup olive oil

½ cup toasted pecans, chopped into
  ¼-inch pieces
½ cup toasted unsalted cashews or
  almonds, chopped into ¼-inch pieces
2½ ounces finely chopped dried figs
2 tablespoons finely chopped celery
2 tablespoons finely chopped red onion
¼ cup finely chopped green onions or
  scallions, green part only

In a large, heavy saucepan, bring the water or stock to the boil. Add the rice, cover, and cook approximately 50 to 60 minutes, or until the rice grains split. *The rice can be refrigerated for 3 days.*

In a blender or food processor, combine the vinegar, lemon juice, garlic, mustard, sugar, salt, and pepper. Process until smooth, then slowly add the vegetable and olive oils to emulsify. *The **dressing can be made 3 or 4 days in advance and refrigerated.***

In a large mixing bowl, toss together the rice, pecans, cashews, figs, celery, red onion, and green onions. Pour enough of the dressing over the rice to coat lightly. Toss well. Serve warm or at room temperature.

Serves 6 to 8

MARJORIE NUNN'S
COUSCOUS SALAD

My friend Marjorie Nunn works long hours and yet entertains fabulously. This is her never-fail recipe that she makes ahead to tote to Symphony in the Park. The salad can be refrigerated for up to 2 days or can stand at room temperature for up to 4 hours.

2 tablespoons wine vinegar	*4 radishes, finely chopped*
2 tablespoons lime juice	*¾ cup finely chopped parsley*
¼ cup olive oil	*½ cup finely chopped mint leaves*
Salt	*½ cup finely chopped celery*
Freshly ground black pepper	*½ cup finely chopped toasted walnuts*
2 cups instant couscous	*4 to 6 scallions, green and white parts,*
2 cups boiling water	*finely chopped*

   In a small mixing bowl, whisk together the vinegar, lime juice, and olive oil. Season to taste with salt and pepper.

   Place the couscous in a medium heatproof bowl. Add the boiling water, stir once, then cover and set aside for 10 minutes. Fluff the couscous with a fork, then add the radishes, parsley, mint, celery, walnuts, and scallions and toss to combine. Add the dressing and toss again.

Serves 4 to 6

SAVANNAH WALKER'S
CANDIED APPLE SALAD

Once Savannah Walker confessed this recipe's secret ingredients, I was surprised at how much I liked it, as I'd not used candy in a congealed salad before! But I enjoyed it that hot Sunday as a side dish, and I've served it often to the after-church crowd with much success. Since that time a few famous chefs (even Paul Prudhomme) have confessed they've used Red-Hots in their recipes. This keeps refrigerated up to 4 days.

½ cup Red-Hots	¼ cup heavy cream
2 cups boiling water	2 tablespoons mayonnaise or salad
2 packages lemon gelatin	dressing
2 cups applesauce	1 head leaf or red lettuce
1 8-ounce package cream cheese, softened	(optional)

In a Pyrex bread pan or bowl, dissolve the Red-Hots in the boiling water. Stir in the gelatin and the applesauce. Chill until partially jelled.

In a separate bowl, combine the cream cheese, cream, and mayonnaise until smooth. Spoon the creamy mixture over the gelatin and rechill until set. Remove the mold from the bowl by inverting the bowl onto a lightly oiled plate. Serve solo or on a bed of lettuce.

Serves 8

AVOCADO-ORANGE SALAD

I love the pale green color and soft smooth texture of a ripe avocado. It's particularly refreshing and pretty in combination with thinly sliced oranges and a light vinaigrette—an excellent companion to Chicken Couscous with Harissa (page 98).

6 large lettuce or spinach leaves, washed	2 avocados, peeled, halved, and sliced
6 large navel oranges, peeled and thinly	Basic Vinaigrette (page 149)
sliced into wagon wheels	

Arrange the lettuce leaves on salad plates. Top with the orange slices and avocado slices. **The salad can be refrigerated at this point for an hour or 2.** Just before serving drizzle the salads with vinaigrette, using about 1 tablespoon per serving.

Serves 4 to 6

RADICCHIO AND GRAPEFRUIT SALAD

 This combination of bitter greens and grapefruit cuts through a rich meal.

8 cups torn salad greens (Boston,
  romaine, red leaf)
2 heads radicchio, separated into leaves
2 heads Belgian endive, separated into
  leaves
1 medium red onion, thinly sliced
2 tablespoons chopped fresh basil
2 pink grapefruits (preferably Ruby
  Red), peeled and cut into segments

VINAIGRETTE
4 tablespoons Dijon mustard
½ cup red wine vinegar
2 tablespoons lime juice
¾ to 1 cup olive oil
2 tablespoons sugar (optional)
Salt
Freshly ground black pepper
4 tablespoons lightly toasted pine nuts or
  chopped walnuts

In a large bowl, toss together the greens, radicchio, endive, onion, basil, and grapefruit segments. In a small bowl, whisk together the mustard, vinegar, lime juice, olive oil, sugar if using, salt, pepper, and pine nuts. *The salad can be refrigerated up to 4 hours.* Just before serving, toss the greens with the dressing.

Serves 6 to 8

PEACH AND MELON MEDLEY

Nothing can top fresh seasonal produce, simply prepared. When the fruits are ripe and juicy and served in a glass bowl or a tall wine goblet to show off their colors, this medley is unbeatable. It would certainly make a lovely dessert, but it's welcome and unexpected as a salad.

4 to 5 large peaches, peeled, pitted, and sliced	1 cantaloupe, cubed
	1 honeydew melon, cubed
Juice and peel (no white attached) of 1 orange, cut into thin julienne strips	3 tablespoons chopped fresh lemon balm or mint
1 to 2 teaspoons sugar (optional)	½ cup sliced toasted almonds (see Note)

In a large bowl, combine the peaches, orange juice and peel, and sugar if using. Chill for at least 30 minutes. **The salad can be prepared to this point up to 2 days in advance**. Combine the melons and lemon balm with the peaches and toss lightly. Sprinkle with the toasted almonds and serve immediately.

Serves 6 to 8

N O T E : *To toast almonds, spread on a metal baking sheet and place in a 300°F. oven for 10 minutes, tossing once or twice, until golden.*

CITRUS, FENNEL, AND PEPPER
SALAD TOPPED WITH FETA

Salads like this one are a real surprise, its unique blend of flavors bringing a flush of unexpected pleasure. It's a good dish year-round, and it can be made a day or so ahead. Use a light or mild olive oil or the oil will dominate the salad. This can be refrigerated up to 4 hours.

2 red grapefruits, peeled and cut into
   segments
2 white grapefruits, peeled and cut into
   segments
2 oranges, peeled and cut into segments
2 small fennel bulbs, core removed, thinly
   sliced
2 red bell peppers, roasted, peeled, seeded, and torn into 1/2-inch strips
1 red onion, halved and thinly sliced

2 tablespoons olive oil or vegetable oil
2 tablespoons fresh lime juice
Grated peel (no white attached) of 1 lime
1 large garlic clove, peeled and chopped
Sugar
Salt
Freshly ground black pepper
1/2 cup crumbled feta cheese
2 green onions, chopped
2 teaspoons chopped fresh thyme leaves

Combine the grapefruit and orange sections, fennel, red peppers, and sliced onion in a large bowl. In a small bowl, mix the oil, lime juice, lime peel, and garlic. Pour the dressing over the fruit mixture and toss to coat. Add sugar, salt, and pepper to taste. Toss and sprinkle the salad with the feta cheese, green onions, and thyme. Cover tightly with plastic wrap and refrigerate for at least an hour. Serve cold.

Serves 4 to 6

Patti's Baked Crab Appetizer ■ Torta Rustica ■ Cucumbers
and Radishes with Yogurt Dip ■ Yogurt Cheese ■ Paula
Wolfert's Artichokes Istanbul Style ■ Eggplant Caponata

APPETIZERS
& STARTERS

■ Spicy Eggplant Spread ■ Poor Man's "Guacamole"
■ Lemon-Pesto Cream Cheese Spread ■ Salmon Dip
or Filling ■ Layered Greek Dip with Pita Wedges

ON A TRULY HECTIC DAY when just getting dinner on the table seems like an insurmountable challenge, you might be tempted to dispense with appetizers or a first course altogether. But resist that temptation; any dish that is so versatile and adds so much to a meal or gathering should not be underestimated.

More than likely these days, the "appetizer" or hors d'oeuvre is served with drinks or functions as a late afternoon or early evening snack, with the main course and dessert served a bit later. Offering these delightful tidbits to the hungry hordes gives me a chance to unwind and talk with friends and family in my kitchen, while I put the finishing touches on the meal and at the same time quell their hunger pangs. My parties frequently feature a number of appetizers, which I spread out on the table as a delicious mishmash that my guests love. Some of my favorites are those that can be served at room temperature and nibbled at throughout the afternoon, as well as those that do double duty, like the Spicy Eggplant Spread that can be reheated and served as a side dish the following day.

When I want to have a starter dish, I find it easiest to get the main course cooking, then turn my attention to the appetizer, combining all these simple ingredients and getting them in the oven, timed for when guests arrive. And when time is truly at a premium, both the pantry and the freezer can provide quick, last-minute starters that I've stashed away for a rainy day.

PATTI'S BAKED
CRAB APPETIZER

Patti was a noncook who started working for me one day a week with the hopes she'd learn to enjoy cooking more. Now she is a great cook and loves it. This is a recipe her grandmother always served at Christmas. I've used it as a hot luncheon dish as well. The best, fresh crabmeat makes this an extraordinary appetizer with the clean sea flavor of the crab, but I confess I've used pasteurized and canned crab when desperate.

1 pound lump backfin crabmeat	1 tablespoon fresh lemon juice
1 tablespoon prepared horseradish	1 cup mayonnaise
¼ cup drained capers	1 egg
2 teaspoons grated lemon peel (no white attached)	Salt
	Freshly ground black pepper
2 teaspoons Worcestershire sauce	2 cups grated sharp Cheddar cheese
½ to 1 teaspoon Tabasco sauce	

Preheat the oven to 350°F.

Mix together the crabmeat, horseradish, capers, lemon peel, Worcestershire sauce, Tabasco, lemon juice, mayonnaise, egg, and salt and pepper to taste. Add 1¼ cups of the cheese to the mixture and mix thoroughly. Spread the mixture evenly in a buttered 10-inch Pyrex plate. *This can be done ahead of time and kept refrigerated for several hours*. When ready to serve, top with the remaining ¾ cup cheese and bake 20 to 25 minutes, until the mixture bubbles. If desired, run under the broiler about 2 minutes to brown on top. Serve with crackers.

Serves 4 to 6

N O T E : *If you want to make individual servings, divide the mixture among 6 buttered glass bowls or ramekins and top with cheese. Place the bowls on a cookie sheet and bake until the mixture bubbles, about 10 to 15 minutes*

TORTA RUSTICA

This is very pretty, and it makes an enormous hit as an appetizer at cocktail parties or even as a main course for a picnic. Since the finished torta freezes up to 4 months, I can make it well in advance of needing it. Make the filling while the dough is rising, and if you don't have time to complete the torta in one day, refrigerate the dough and filling separately and then combine and bake the next day.

GARLIC SHORT CUTS
Chop several cloves of garlic and place in a jar with oil to cover. They should be kept in the refrigerator until needed. Measure out and drain off oil. As a rule of thumb, I use 1 teaspoon of chopped garlic for each chopped garlic clove called for in a recipe, but you may want to adjust the amount more or less according to your palate.

1 package active dry yeast
1 tablespoon sugar
¼ cup warm water (105°F. to 115°F.)
1 egg
¼ cup milk
3 tablespoons olive oil
2 teaspoons salt
3 cups bread flour

½ pound hot Italian sausage
½ pound mild Italian sausage
¼ cup butter or oil, if needed
2 medium onions, chopped
2 to 3 garlic cloves, peeled and finely
   chopped
2 tablespoons finely chopped fresh basil

2 teaspoons fennel seeds
2 teaspoons chopped fresh thyme or 1
   teaspoon dried
3 eggs, lightly beaten
1 15-ounce container ricotta cheese
½ cup freshly grated imported Parmesan
   cheese
2 10-ounce packages frozen spinach,
   thawed and well drained
1 1-pound can Italian tomatoes, drained
   and coarsely chopped
Salt
Freshly ground black pepper

G L A Z E
1 egg beaten with 1 teaspoon water

In a small bowl, dissolve the yeast and sugar in the water. Whisk together the egg, milk, and olive oil and stir into the yeast mixture. Add the salt, then stir in the flour 1 cup at a time to make a stiff dough. Knead until elastic and smooth as a baby's bottom, 1 minute in a food processor, 10 minutes in a mixer or by hand. Place the dough in an oiled plastic bag or oiled bowl and turn to coat on all sides. Seal or cover with plastic wrap. Let rise until doubled, about 1 hour.

Meanwhile, heat a large skillet, prick the sausages, and add to the pan. If after a few minutes they are sticking as there is not enough fat to fry them, add 1 to 2 tablespoons butter or oil to the pan. Fry until done. Remove them with a slotted spoon and slice about ¼ inch thick. Add more butter or oil if needed to cook the onions. Add the onions and garlic to the skillet and cook until soft, about 5 minutes. Remove from the heat and cool slightly. Add the basil, fennel seeds, thyme, eggs, ricotta, Parmesan, spinach, and tomatoes. Stir in the sliced sausage and combine well. Taste and season well with salt and pepper. *The filling can be refrigerated for 24 hours.*

Preheat the oven to 375°F. Oil a 10-inch springform pan. Roll the dough out into a circle, about 18 to 20 inches in diameter. Lay the dough gently onto the prepared pan, letting the excess hang out evenly around the pan. Spread the filling evenly in the pan. Fold the overhanging dough in toward the center and gather it into a decorative shape. Brush with the egg glaze. Bake for approximately 1½ to 1¾ hours, or until golden. Let cool and serve at room temperature.

Serves 8 to 10 as an appetizer

CUCUMBERS AND RADISHES WITH YOGURT DIP

This make-ahead dip makes a cool, refreshing start to a summer barbecue, followed by kebabs and couscous. The green, red, and white presentation is as colorful as the Italian flag!

½ cup lowfat yogurt, well drained
½ cup sour cream
¾ teaspoon ground cumin
¾ teaspoon ground coriander
Salt

Freshly ground black pepper
1½ tablespoons finely chopped fresh mint
2 cucumbers, unpeeled, scored, and cut
    into ¼-inch slices
10 to 12 radishes, washed and trimmed

In a mixing bowl, combine the yogurt, sour cream, cumin, coriander, salt and pepper to taste, and mint and whisk until well combined. Place in the refrigerator and chill at least 1 to 2 hours, preferably overnight. Serve with the cucumbers and radishes for dipping.

Serves 6

YOGURT CHEESE

This cheese has become a staple in my home. It makes a good substitute for cream cheese, with a real saving in calories and fat. You can use plain, lowfat, or nonfat yogurt—it's your choice.

2 16-ounce containers plain yogurt

Rinse and squeeze dry a large piece of cheesecloth. Double it and line a strainer with the cloth. Put the yogurt in the center. Fold over any excess cloth to cover. Set the strainer over a bowl and let it drain overnight in the refrigerator. Scrape the cheese into a covered container. The final amount will depend on how much liquid there is in the yogurt.

Makes approximately 2 cups

PAULA WOLFERT'S ARTICHOKES ISTANBUL STYLE

This dish is a great favorite in Istanbul. Long, slow cooking is the key to the silky artichokes, and since this improves with age, it should be made about 5 hours in advance. Serve it as a first course or even as the centerpiece of a vegetarian meal. Don't omit the sugar or the sauce will not have the right heftiness.

3 lemons
2 tablespoons all-purpose flour
1 teaspoon salt
6 fresh artichokes
2 thin carrots, pared and cut into 1-inch lengths, or 1 celery stalk, stringed and cut into 1-inch pieces

1 medium potato, peeled and cut into wedges
10 shallots, peeled
2½ teaspoons sugar
⅓ cup extra-virgin olive oil
¼ to ½ cup snipped fresh dill
2 lemons, cut into quarters

Preheat the oven to 300°F.

Juice the lemons and set the shells aside for later use. In a deep bowl, combine 1 quart water, the flour, ½ teaspoon salt, and 2 tablespoons lemon juice. Trim the artichokes, rub with a juiced lemon half, and immediately place in the bowl.

Put the artichokes, stems up, carrots or celery, potato wedges, shallots, and 1 cup of the flour-water mixture in a wide casserole that can go over the heat. Add ½ cup water, the sugar, 3 tablespoons lemon juice, the olive oil, and the remaining ½ teaspoon salt. Bring to the boil and allow the liquid to boil vigorously for 1 minute. Cover with 1 sheet of moistened and crumpled parchment paper and a tight-fitting lid and place the casserole in the oven to cook for 1½ hours.

Remove from the oven and let cool before removing the artichokes from the casserole. Serve the artichokes with the syrupy juices and a light dusting of snipped dill. Garnish with the lemon quarters.

Serves 6

EGGPLANT CAPONATA

Caponata is a traditional Sicilian dish composed of eggplant in a sweet-and-sour sauce that is often garnished with slices of smoked fish. The carrots add a nontraditional sweetness to this version. I enjoy it cold on a picnic or served at room temperature as much as I do when it is hot. It also serves well as a bed for roast beef, lamb, or poultry. For instant bruschetta, spread on French bread and broil about 2 minutes. If time allows, sprinkle the eggplants with salt, place in a colander for 30 minutes, rinse, and pat dry. This can be refrigerated for up to 4 days. Allow the caponata to return to room temperature before serving.

⅔ cup olive oil	⅓ cup red wine vinegar
3 eggplants, sliced lengthwise ¼ inch thick	2 tablespoons chopped fresh basil
2 red onions, sliced	2 tablespoons chopped fresh or dried oregano
6 green onions, chopped	3 tablespoons drained capers
10 garlic cloves, peeled and sliced	1 to 2 tablespoons sugar
2 red peppers, seeded and sliced	Salt
2 green peppers, seeded and sliced	Freshly ground black pepper
4 carrots, shredded	¾ to 1 cup freshly grated imported

Heat ⅓ cup of the olive oil in a large (5-quart) Dutch oven. Add the eggplant slices, red onions, green onions, garlic slices, red and green peppers, and carrots. Cook, stirring constantly, over high heat until the vegetables begin to brown slightly, about 15 minutes. Transfer to a glass bowl. In a measuring cup, whisk together the remaining olive oil, red wine vinegar, basil, oregano, capers, and sugar. Add to the vegetables. Season to taste with salt and pepper and top with the Parmesan.

Serves 8 to 10

KNIVES

The most important thing about knives is to keep them sharp. You have to use more force with a dull knife, which is tiring, and a dull knife is more apt to slip, which can be dangerous to your fingers. Use a "sharpening" steel occasionally while you are cutting. The steel does not actually sharpen the blade; it resets the edge. The result is much the same, however. If your knives get heavy use, invest in a quality electric sharpener to touch them up every couple of months.

Use a knife that fits your hand and that fits the job. Don't try to whittle through a large roast with a paring knife. On the other hand, it would be awkward to use a butcher's knife or a large chef's knife to carve a tomato rose.

Hold a chef's knife close to the heel of the blade. This position takes advantage of the balance of the knife. Don't extend your forefinger along the back of the blade—you lose some control and the position is tiring.

Although we talk about *chopping* an onion, herbs, and the

SPICY EGGPLANT SPREAD

Cocktail party food needs a lot of character to hold its own. This spicy spread more than does that. It may be served warm as a side dish, or at room temperature or cold as an appetizer accompanied by pita wedges (page 56). Not only may the whole dish be cooked in stages as below, it may also be made several days in advance.

This originated as a side dish for a lamb dish. I reheated it next (to rave reviews!), and the third time around it became a chilled spread for crackers. The recipe doubles easily.

1 2-pound eggplant, halved	1 teaspoon turmeric
2 tablespoons oil	1 teaspoon sugar
2 medium onions, cut into 1/2-inch cubes	1/4 cup yogurt
2 garlic cloves, peeled and finely chopped	Salt
2 teaspoons ground coriander seeds	Freshly ground black pepper

Preheat the oven to 400° F.

Place the eggplant, cut-side down, on a foil-lined baking sheet. Bake 30 to 45 minutes, or until soft. Remove from the oven and set aside to cool. Alternatively, you can grill the eggplant over hot coals. When cool enough to handle, peel and cut the pulp into large chunks. *This can be done a day or 2 in advance and kept in the refrigerator.*

Heat the oil in a large saucepan over medium-high heat. Add the onions and cook 2 to 3 minutes. Then add the garlic and continue cooking until soft but not brown, about 2 minutes. Add the eggplant, coriander, turmeric, and sugar. Cook until soft and well combined, about 5 to 10 minutes. Stir in the yogurt and season generously with salt and pepper. Serve hot, warm, or at room temperature.

Makes 2 to 2 1/2 cups

POOR MAN'S "GUACAMOLE"

This "guacamole" tastes surprisingly like the real thing. It is virtually fat-free if you leave out the olive oil and use a nonfat yogurt. Serve with pita wedges or the traditional tortilla chips. It can be made ahead but will become watery after 2 days.

6 firm zucchini, grated
1 cup Yogurt Cheese (page 50)
1 red onion, chopped
3 garlic cloves, peeled and chopped
1 to 2 jalapeño peppers, chopped
3 tablespoons chopped fresh cilantro

2 tablespoons white wine vinegar
2 tablespoons Dijon mustard
2 tablespoons olive oil (optional)
2 tomatoes, chopped (reserve ¼ cup for garnish)
2 green onions, chopped

Place the zucchini in a large skillet, and quickly stir-fry over high heat until they just begin to wilt, about 2 to 3 minutes. Drain on paper towels to remove the excess liquid.

In a large bowl, combine the Yogurt Cheese, red onion, garlic, jalapeño peppers, cilantro, vinegar, mustard, olive oil if using, and tomatoes. Add the wilted zucchini mixture. Mix very well and top with the remaining chopped tomatoes and the green onions. Chill 2 to 3 hours before serving.

Makes 2 to 3 cups

NOTE: *A food processor really speeds up this dish. With the steel knife, first chop the herbs, then the garlic, followed by the peppers, then the onions. Grate the zucchini last, in the already dirty bowl, using the large grating blade or the julienne blade. If you don't have a food processor, use a hand grater.*

LEMON–PESTO CREAM CHEESE SPREAD

PHYLLO BASKETS
You can make lovely pastry baskets with phyllo dough (see page 176 for basic instructions). Lay out a sheet of phyllo and brush it with clarified butter. Repeat twice for a stack of 3 buttered sheets. Cut the stack into 24 squares, 6 down and 4 across. Press one stacked square into a muffin tin. Bake at 375° F. for 8 to 10 minutes. Cool on a rack. You can store them in an airtight container at room temperature for a couple of days or freeze them up to 6 months. Make sure the container is rigid enough to protect the baskets.

This tasty filling for nibbling goes in Phyllo Baskets (see sidebar) or can be spread on crackers or pita wedges. Thinned with yogurt, it can be used as a dip. It may be made up to 3 days in advance and kept in the refrigerator.

3 8-ounce packages cream cheese, softened
1 cup Pesto Sauce (page 155)

Grated peel (no white attached) and juice of 2 lemons

In a food processor, combine the cream cheese, pesto, lemon peel, and lemon juice. Process until just combined. Chill and serve cold.

Makes about 4 cups

SALMON DIP OR FILLING

An easy hors d'oeuvre that is extremely delicious, this may be made ahead one or two days. For really smashing party fare, pipe the filling into Phyllo Baskets (see sidebar).

3 8-ounce packages cream cheese
½ pound smoked salmon
Juice of 2 limes

10 to 12 green onions, sliced, including green tops
2 to 3 tablespoons chopped fresh dill

Place the cream cheese and salmon in the bowl of a blender or food processor and process until just combined. Add the lime juice, green onions, and fresh dill and pulse 4 to 5 times, or until combined but still retaining some texture. Serve with cucumber rounds or crackers.

Makes about 4 cups

LAYERED GREEK DIP
WITH PITA WEDGES

This easy, make-ahead layered dip combines several flavors and textures from the Mediterranean. Serve it in a pretty glass dish to show off the layers and surround with pita wedges. To reduce calories, substitute Yogurt Cheese for the cream cheese. Peperoncini are medium-hot Italian pickled peppers. Not only may the dip be made a day in advance, I chop everything but the tomato several days ahead of time, refrigerate the ingredients in plastic bags, and combine them the day before the party. I do this as much to save refrigerator space as to save time.

1 8-ounce package cream cheese, softened, or 1 cup Yogurt Cheese (page 50)
1½ cups sour cream
1⅓ cups canned or cooked artichoke hearts, chopped
8 peperoncini peppers, seeded and chopped
4 hard-cooked eggs, chopped
16 black Greek olives, pitted and halved
Juice of 1 lemon

1 tablespoon chopped fresh oregano
2 tablespoons drained capers
16 green Greek olives, pitted and halved
1 large tomato, chopped
3 garlic cloves, peeled and chopped
1 small cucumber, finely chopped
4 ounces feta cheese, crumbled
1 red bell pepper, seeded and chopped
2 tablespoons chopped fresh parsley
Pita wedges (see sidebar)

In a bowl, combine the cream cheese, ½ cup of the sour cream, and half the chopped artichoke hearts. Spread the mixture evenly in the bottom of a clear glass 1½-quart serving bowl. Mix together the peperoncini peppers, eggs, and black olives and add as the next layer. Combine the remaining 1 cup sour cream, lemon juice, and oregano and spread this evenly over the pepper layer. Sprinkle the capers over this layer. Then layer the green olives, tomato, garlic, cucumber, remaining artichoke hearts, feta cheese, red pepper, and parsley. Cover with plastic wrap and chill 8 hours to overnight. Serve with pita wedges.

Serves 8 to 10

Beef Rib Eye Roast with Savory Sauce ■ Lemon-Rosemary
Standing Rib Roast ■ Alma's Brisket and Limas One-Pot Meal
■ Cajun Country Meat Loaf ■ Tuscan Lemon Beef ■ Pot Roast
with Lemon, Onions, and Prunes ■ Mimi's Flank Steak ■
Bolognese Meat Sauce ■ Cold Fillet of Beef with Green
Peppercorn Sauce ■ Slow Roast Beef with Basil Lemon Vegetables
■ Ginger-Mint Leg of Lamb ■ Braised Lamb with Carrots ■

MEAT 3 DISHES

Grecian Lamb and Eggplant Casserole ■ Lamb with Preserved
Lemons ■ Lamb and Italian Sausage Stew ■ Lamb Chops with
Dijon-Rosemary Crust ■ Versatile Lamb Stuffing ■ Convenience
Cassoulet ■ Home-Style Ham and Potato Casserole ■ Pork with
Almond Crust ■ Barbecued Pork Loin ■ Hoisin and Honey Pork
Loin ■ Pork Loin with Spiced Peach Chutney ■ Root Vegetables
with Pork Tenderloin ■ Fresh Pork Roast with Dried Fruit

I USED TO THINK the only kind of meat dishes that were possible for a busy day were quickly grilled chops or stir-fries. But elegant roasts such as a rib eye or tenderloin of beef, shoulder or leg of lamb, and pork loins and hams (both fresh and cured) are much easier to cook than a steak if you also need to prepare vegetables and get everything to come out at the same time.

I remember the first roast I fixed as a young bride over thirty years ago. I invited my best friend's parents and the Van den Bergs, who were like second parents to me. The beef terrified me, as I had never roasted a large piece of meat before. I rubbed it with seasonings and put it in the oven, set the timer, and sat back, incredulous that this was all there was to it. It gave me time to set the table, do my hair, and be completely relaxed when my guests arrived. I thought it was miraculous.

Certain cuts of meat lend themselves to long, slow cooking, whether as roasts or as stews. These are usually the most flavorful and less tender cuts such as chuck, brisket, and round beef. Ground meat can also take a long cooking, either in the Bolognese Meat Sauce (which cooks unattended all day) or a savory meat loaf, which is cooked, like a roast, according to weight.

And another advantage of cooking a large piece of meat or batch of stew not to be overlooked is the bonus of reheatable leftovers, the biggest boon of all to busy cooks.

BEEF RIB EYE ROAST WITH SAVORY SAUCE

A rib eye roast is one of the most impressive pieces of beef to serve. It carves easily, either thinly or thickly, depending on your pocketbook. It is best served after resting 10 minutes from the time it is removed from the oven , but it may be served cold as well.

2 garlic cloves, peeled and finely chopped
1 teaspoon salt
1 teaspoon cracked black pepper
1 teaspoon chopped fresh or dried thyme
   leaves
1 teaspoon chopped fresh or ½ teaspoon
   dried tarragon leaves

1 beef rib eye roast (about 4 pounds)
¼ cup finely chopped shallots
1 cup beef broth
1 tablespoon tomato paste
½ teaspoon sugar (optional)

Preheat the oven to 350°F.

Combine the garlic, salt, pepper, thyme, and tarragon in a small bowl, mixing until a paste is formed. Spread the mixture evenly over the surface of the beef roast. Place it on a rack, fat-side up, in a shallow roasting pan. Do not add water and do not cover. Roast to the desired doneness: 18 to 20 minutes per pound for rare, 20 to 22 minutes per pound for medium. Remove the roast from the oven when a meat thermometer registers 135°F. for rare or 155°F. for medium. Transfer the roast to a carving board and allow it to stand 15 to 20 minutes before carving.

Meanwhile, remove the rack from the roasting pan; drain off the fat. Add the shallots to the cooking juices left in the pan; cook and stir over medium heat for 2 to 3 minutes. Add the broth, tomato paste, and sugar if using. Stir until the meat juices attached to the pan are dissolved. Increase the heat to medium-high and continue cooking until the liquid is reduced to ¾ cup, about 5 to 10 minutes.

Carve the roast across the grain into ¼-inch-thick slices and pass the pan gravy separately.

Serves 8

LEMON-ROSEMARY
STANDING RIB ROAST

I like to pull out all the stops for holidays and a rib roast does this, yet it's so easy—once in the oven it requires no attention. A rib roast may be cooked to your preference but I prefer rare to medium.

A rib roast may be stored in the refrigerator for 3 to 5 days after purchase. For longer storage, freezing is recommended—up to 2 weeks in retail package; for a longer time wrap in foil, freezer paper, or polyethylene film. Defrost in the wrapping 4 to 7 hours for a large roast, 3 to 5 for a small one. A roast from the small end (ribs 11 to 12) is the prettiest, as it does not have a "cap," which needs to be removed.

COOKING TEMPERA-TURES FOR BEEF
Recommended internal temperature for beef:
Rare	140° F.
Medium Rare	150° F.
Medium	160° F.
Well Done	170° F.

2 teaspoons grated lemon peel (no white attached)	*1 teaspoon dried rosemary leaves*
2 garlic cloves, peeled and chopped	*1 teaspoon salt*
1 teaspoon cracked black pepper	*1 4- to 6-pound rib roast*

Preheat the oven to 325°F.

In a small bowl, mix together the lemon peel, garlic, black pepper, rosemary, and salt. Pat evenly over the roast. Place it, fat-side up on a rack in an open roasting pan. Roast 26 to 30 minutes per pound for a rare roast, 34 to 38 minutes per pound for medium. (For a 6- to 8-pound roast, roast 23 to 25 minutes per pound for rare, 27 to 30 minutes per pound for medium.) A meat thermometer should register 5 to 10 degrees below the desired temperature, since the internal temperature will continue to rise 5 to 10 degrees after you remove it from the oven. Allow the roast to stand, tented with foil, 15 to 20 minutes before carving.

Serves 8 to 10

ALMA'S BRISKET AND LIMAS
ONE-POT MEAL

My friend Alma regularly prepares this brisket for her family. She varies it each time—sometimes adding potatoes, carrots, or peas along with or instead of the lima beans. Once the meat is browned, the onions, beans, and herbs have been added, and the brisket is simmering, she is able to go visit her elderly father next door, and then come home and take a nap, all before dinner. After her hard week, she figures she deserves it!

Not only is this brisket better the next day and easier to slice, it also keeps nicely for several days.

1½ cups dried lima beans	Salt
1 2- to 2½-pound brisket	Freshly ground black pepper
3 large onions, chopped	¼ cup brandy or dry sherry
4 cups red or rosé wine, beef stock, or	¼ cup ketchup
water	2 tablespoons red wine vinegar
2 garlic cloves, peeled and chopped	2 tablespoons Worcestershire sauce
2 bay leaves, chopped	2 to 3 cups peeled and chunked vegeta-
1 tablespoon chopped fresh oregano	bles such as carrots, potatoes, beans,
2 tablespoons chopped fresh rosemary	peas, or the like (optional)

In a large bowl, combine the beans with water to cover by an inch or so and soak 4 hours or overnight. Drain and set aside.

Heat a large Dutch oven, add the brisket, brown it on one side, then turn and brown the other. Add the lima beans, onions, wine, garlic, bay leaves, oregano, and rosemary. Bring to the boil, lower the heat, then cover and simmer for 2 hours, or place in a 300°F. oven for 2 hours. ***The brisket can be refrigerated at this point for a day or 2. Bring to the boil on top of the stove before continuing.*** Remove from the heat and season to taste with salt and pepper. Add the brandy, ketchup, vinegar, Worcestershire, and any vegetables if using. Simmer on low heat or return to the slow oven for another hour, or until the vegetables are tender.

Serves 4

CAJUN COUNTRY MEAT LOAF

Meat loaf doesn't take long to put together and then takes its time in the oven. I must admit I love the smell of meat loaf as much as the taste. It's good freshly made, but it's even better the next day, reheated, and leftovers also make wonderful sandwiches. I double the recipe when I am able to and freeze one of the loaves for another time. This is a very good use for leftover cooked rice.

This meat loaf combines what Paul Prudhomme calls the "trinity" of Cajun cooking: onions, garlic, and peppers. The horseradish gives it an extra zing, and you can vary the spiciness with more Tabasco. This freezes for up to 3 months.

1 pound ground beef	1 tablespoon chili powder
1 pound ground pork	2 teaspoons paprika
½ pound hot sausage	1 teaspoon mustard seeds
1 onion, chopped	1 teaspoon ground cumin
3 garlic cloves, peeled and chopped	½ teaspoon fennel seeds
1 carrot, shredded	½ teaspoon cayenne pepper
1 red pepper, chopped	Dash of Tabasco sauce
1 cup cooked rice	Salt
2 eggs	Freshly ground black pepper
½ cup ketchup	2 strips bacon
1 tablespoon Dijon mustard	½ cup ketchup combined with ¼ cup
1 to 2 teaspoons prepared horseradish	beef stock
½ cup breadcrumbs	

Preheat the oven to 375°F. Grease or oil a 9 × 5 × 3-inch pan.

In a large bowl, combine the beef, pork, sausage, onion, garlic, carrot, red pepper, rice, eggs, ketchup, mustard, horseradish, breadcrumbs, chili powder, paprika, mustard seeds, cumin, fennel, cayenne, Tabasco, and salt and pepper. Shape the mixture into a loaf and place in the prepared pan. Top with the bacon strips and bake for 30 minutes. Pour the ketchup and beef stock mixture over the meat, and continue baking 30 to 40 minutes longer. Remove from the oven and let cool in the pan 10 minutes before slicing.

Serves 6 to 8

TUSCAN LEMON BEEF

I was served this on a recent trip to Italy. It is a marvelous way to cook an inexpensive, lean piece of meat. It is moist and tender, with enormous flavor. This can be frozen for up to 4 months.

2 pounds eye of round beef
3 onions, quartered
3 carrots, cut into 3-inch pieces
2 celery stalks, without leaves, cut into
3-inch pieces

Grated peel (no white attached) and juice
of 3 large lemons
2 cups milk

Preheat the oven to 250° F.

Place the meat in a medium-size heavy casserole. Add the onions, carrots, celery, and lemon peel and juice. Cover tightly and place in the oven. Cook for 3 hours. Remove from the oven, remove the cover, add the milk, and let cook, uncovered, in the oven 1 more hour, or until the milk has nearly evaporated. Remove the meat to a serving platter and slice. Puree the onions, carrots, celery, lemon peel, and any remaining juice. Spoon the puree over the meat.

Serves 6

POT ROAST WITH LEMON, ONIONS, AND PRUNES

One of the virtues of pot roasts is that they may be eaten right away or kept for several days in the refrigerator. Another virtue of this one is that it may be cooked in stages if time is limited. Its long, slow bake ensures moistness.

So very tasty, the lemon and prunes in this dish add a lovely sweet tartness. It's a marvelously unusual sauce. A friend's mother always added a cinnamon stick to her pot roast, a trick I've adopted here.

1 2½- to 3½-pound brisket or chuck roast
Grated peel (no white attached) and juice of 1 lemon
1½ to 2 cups fresh or canned stock or broth (a combination of beef and chicken if nice is using canned)
1 tablespoon honey
1 tablespoon cider vinegar
Pinch of ground cloves
¼ teaspoon ground cinnamon
6 to 8 carrots, peeled and cut into 5- or 6-inch lengths
2 to 3 large onions, peeled and quartered
1 cup pitted prunes
1 tablespoon cornstarch
1 tablespoon water

Preheat the oven to 300°F.

Trim most of the excess fat from the meat. Heat a large ovenproof casserole that is large enough to hold the brisket when flat. Add the brisket, fat-side down, to the hot pan. Brown the meat over high heat, then turn and brown the second side. Pour the lemon juice and peel around the meat, add the stock, then cover and bake for 1½ hours. Remove from the oven. *The pot roast can be refrigerated at this point for a day or two. Bring to the boil on top of the stove before continuing.*

Mix together the honey, vinegar, cloves, and cinnamon and add to the pan juices. Arrange the carrots, onions, and prunes around the meat. Cover, return to the oven, and bake 1½ hours, until tender.

Transfer the meat and vegetables to a platter with a slotted spoon. On top of the stove, combine the cornstarch and water and slowly whisk into the pan juices. Bring to the boil and cook, stirring, over medium heat until slightly thickened, 3 to 4 minutes. Spoon over meat and vegetables.

Serves 6 to 8

MIMI'S FLANK STEAK

Mimi, who has been my housemate for the last three years, is always in a hurry. She has a high-powered job, a boyfriend, and a multitude of activities. When she cooks at home, it's always fast, easy, and full of flavor, like this tasty marinated steak. This recipe was her mother's, and she knows it like the back of her hand. Leftovers are great served at room temperature.

½ cup soy sauce
3 tablespoons Dijon mustard
1 tablespoon freshly ground black pepper

4 garlic cloves, peeled and chopped
¼ cup Worcestershire sauce
1 2- to 2½-pound flank steak

In a small bowl, whisk together the soy sauce, mustard, pepper, garlic, and Worcestershire sauce. Pour over the flank steak and marinate in the refrigerator 6 hours or up to 2 days.

Remove the steak from the marinade and grill or broil 6 inches from the heat 7 minutes on each side. Let the steak sit 10 minutes before slicing thinly on the diagonal.

Serves 4

BOLOGNESE MEAT SAUCE

I made my first trip to Italy in 1971. It was a radiant trip because it cast light on one of the finest cuisines in the world. I remember sitting in a workingman's café in Bologna, eating this sauce, trying to relate it to the long-cooking spaghetti sauces of my childhood, as it is pale pink, meaty, and in fact really has very little of what we think of as sauce. According to Marcella Hazan, who opened my eyes even more to the cooking of this region through her books and classes, Bolognese sauce is not traditionally served on spaghetti at all, but on any one of a number of pastas. Purists will applaud the addition of milk, which, as I learned from Marcella, tempers the acidity, and will decry the garlic and sugar, which I feel rounds it out further.

This sauce cooks with little attention for a minimum of 3 hours. It likes even more time and needs a large, heavy pot. This makes 2 meals for 4 to 6 people. I usually serve one batch and freeze one.

If possible, reduce the wine and tomatoes and their juice separately. But if you have little time to watch, add them together after the milk has boiled away completely. The liquid in the sauce is nearly completely gone, with the meat and fat coating the pasta as a butter sauce would. It freezes for up to 3 months.

TO COOK PASTA AHEAD OF TIME
For a quick meal, pasta is the thing that takes the most time. It's the boiling of the water—which can take 20 minutes to half an hour—that is the most irritating to wait for. After all, boiling water doesn't even smell good! I do have an instant hot water dispenser on my sink, which I wouldn't trade for anything. I often cook pasta a pound at a time, saving half for a second meal, although I wouldn't invite an Italian like Marcella Hazan or Giuliano Bugialli to dinner when I did this. I refrigerate it in an airtight container or plastic bag and reheat it by microwaving it, by dipping it in boiling water and then draining immediately, or by tossing it in a frying pan with hot oil or butter until coated and heated through. And there is always pasta salad.

3 tablespoons oil	⅛ teaspoon freshly grated nutmeg
5 tablespoons butter	2 cups dry white wine
2 medium onions, chopped	1 28-ounce can Italian plum tomatoes,
2 garlic cloves, peeled and chopped	cut up, with their juice
2 celery stalks, chopped	Sugar (optional)
2 carrots, chopped	Salt
1½ pounds ground chuck	3 pounds pasta (1 pound for 4 people)—
1½ cups milk	tortellini, rigatoni, conchiglie, fusilli
Freshly ground black pepper	Freshly grated imported Parmesan cheese

In a large pot, heat the oil and 3 tablespoons of the butter. Add the onions and cook until soft, about 5 minutes. Add the garlic, celery, and carrots and cook, stirring, 2 or 3 minutes. Crumble the beef into the pot and cook, stirring as needed, until the beef starts to turn white, 4 to 5 minutes. Add the milk, bring to the boil, reduce the heat, and simmer until the milk has evaporated. Add the freshly ground pepper and grate the nutmeg in. Add the wine, bring to the boil, reduce, and simmer until it is evaporated, about 10 minutes. Stir in the tomatoes, bring back to the boil, and reduce the heat. Cook over very low heat, uncovered, until the liquid is evaporated, about 10 to 15 minutes. *You can stop at this point or any point from now on, returning the sauce to the boil, then lowering the heat to a simmer, and continuing the process. I've done this over several days but it really is best when finished the first day*. This reduction usually takes a couple of hours. Add a cup of water, stir, and let simmer again. Repeat this process until the mixture has cooked 3 to 4 hours. The fat will rise to the surface and separate and this is necessary to coat the pasta. Taste and add sugar if using, and salt and pepper as needed.

When ready to eat, toss the hot sauce with the cooked, drained pasta, the remaining 2 tablespoons butter, and the freshly grated Parmesan. The sauce will keep, refrigerated, 2 to 3 days.

Makes 2 batches for 4 to 6

COLD FILLET OF BEEF WITH GREEN PEPPERCORN SAUCE

This is a perfect dish for a buffet or luncheon because it can be cooked several days ahead and served chilled or at room temperature. The lively green sauce will keep for a least a week in the refrigerator and is excellent on cold poached salmon as well. Try the sauce over summer-ripe tomatoes for an unusual salad.

BEEF YIELDS
Different cuts of meat will yield a different number of servings, pound for pound. For example, a beef rib eye roast will yield about 3½ 3-ounce cooked, trimmed servings per pound. And figure 2 servings per pound of uncooked bone-in meat.

1 4- to 5-pound whole beef tenderloin, trimmed of all visible fat
2 tablespoons olive oil
Salt
Freshly ground black pepper

GREEN PEPPERCORN SAUCE
3 tablespoons chopped fresh parsley
3 tablespoons chopped fresh basil
3 tablespoons chopped fresh sorrel (optional)

5 small gherkin pickles
2 tablespoons drained capers
4 anchovy fillets
2 green onions
4 garlic cloves, peeled
2 tablespoons lemon juice
2 tablespoons grated lemon peel (no white attached)
2 tablespoons Dijon mustard
3 to 4 teaspoons drained green peppercorns in brine
1 cup olive oil

Preheat the oven to 500°F.

Rub the meat with the oil and salt and pepper to taste. Place the tenderloin, tail tucked under, in a shallow baking dish or broiler pan. Bake 30 minutes, or until a meat thermometer registers 140°F. for rare. Remove from the oven, cool, and slice thinly. *The beef can be refrigerated for 2 or 3 days.*

Make the sauce by combining the parsley, basil, sorrel if using, pickles, capers, anchovies, green onions, garlic, lemon juice, lemon peel, mustard, and peppercorns in a food processor or blender. Puree until smooth. Add the olive oil in a slow, steady stream to the puree, blending until thick and creamy. *The dressing can be made several days in advance*. Serve with the cold beef.

Serves 10 to 12

SLOW ROAST BEEF WITH BASIL LEMON VEGETABLES

**LETTING
MEAT REST**
It is important to let a
roast—beef, pork, lamb,
poultry, or the like—
rest before you carve it.
First, the outer sections
of the meat are hotter
than the center and
resting will allow the
temperature to even
out. Second, some of
the juices can retreat
back into the meat. If
you carve a roast too
soon, you will lose
much of its juice to the
carving board.

All in one, this colorful casserole is incredibly fresh tasting and very up to the minute, with the meat coming out slightly pink inside, brown outside. The flavor of the basil leaves permeates both the vegetables and the meat. Whole or cut-up chicken or Cornish hen could easily be substituted for the meat. There will be a considerable amount of juices left in the bag and pan; they can be used to make couscous or rice.

2 tablespoons flour
2 zucchini, sliced
2 yellow squash, sliced
1 onion, sliced
½ eggplant, sliced
2 garlic cloves, peeled and chopped
Salt
Freshly ground black pepper
1 tablespoon lemon pepper (optional)
Grated peel (no white attached) of
　1 lemon

10 whole basil leaves
1 2½-pound chuck, sirloin tip or round
　roast

GARNISH
3 tablespoons chopped fresh basil
1 garlic clove, peeled and chopped
Grated peel (no white attached) of
　1 lemon

Place a large roasting bag in a large roasting pan. Dust the insides of the bag with the flour, shaking if necessary. Add the zucchini, squash, onion, eggplant, garlic, salt, pepper, and lemon pepper to taste if using. Add the peel, toss to mix, and then spread out inside the bag. Arrange the basil leaves evenly over the vegetables. Rub the roast with the lemon pepper if using, or salt and pepper. Place it on top of the basil and vegetables. Seal the bag and roast for 2½ hours.

Remove the roast and let rest 10 minutes. Slice thinly across the grain. Arrange the slices on a platter, and surround with the vegetables. (The whole basil may be discarded.)

For the garnish, mix together the basil, garlic, and lemon peel and sprinkle over the vegetables.

Serves 4

GINGER-MINT LEG OF LAMB

This lamb dish uses minimal fat but cooks up juicy and tender. It takes little effort to prepare the marinade, which imparts a taste that is light and tangy with a distinct Indian flair. Serve the lamb with a cold cucumber chutney and couscous in warm weather or a hot chutney and rice for cold winter fare.

1 5- to 6-pound leg of lamb	1 tablespoon paprika
	1 tablespoon ground cumin
MARINADE	½ teaspoon ground cloves
2 tablespoons finely chopped garlic	½ teaspoon kosher salt
2 tablespoons finely chopped fresh ginger	¼ cup vegetable oil
3 tablespoons finely chopped fresh mint	3 tablespoons fresh lemon juice

Before marinating the lamb, trim off all visible fat. To prepare the marinade, combine the garlic, ginger, mint, paprika, cumin, cloves, salt, oil, and lemon juice together in a small bowl. Place the leg of lamb in a 9½ × 13½-inch baking dish and pour the marinade mixture over the leg, rubbing it in, and turning to cover. Cover the meat with plastic wrap and let it stand in the marinade for at least 4 hours and up to 2 days in the refrigerator, turning several times.

When ready to cook the lamb, preheat the oven to 400°F. Place the pan with the meat and marinade in the oven and roast for 15 minutes, then reduce the oven temperature to 300°F. and cook 2½ hours longer, turning the lamb after an hour or so. A meat thermometer should read 155°F. at the thickest part of the meat for medium rare.

Let the meat rest for 10 or 15 minutes, then slice thinly and serve with the pan juices.

Serves 8

BAKED POTATOES
A baked potato is an excellent accompaniment for many main dishes, but it is also a great main course itself. My sister often has a baked potato and a green salad for a light meal. Yes, a light meal. An 8-ounce baked potato has only about 160 calories. It's the added butter, sour cream, cheese, bacon, and the like that make the calorie count climb out of sight.

Simply prick the potato several times with a fork and bake at 500°F. for about 1 to 1½ hours. It will bake perfectly well at a lower temperature for a longer time. You can also rub the potato with a little oil or butter before baking for a softer skin.

BRAISED LAMB WITH CARROTS

**TO COOK
RICE AHEAD
OF TIME**
Rice can be cooked,
frozen, and reheated, if
cooked properly the
first time. To cook,
bring a large pot of
water with a dash of
salt to the boil. Add the
rice and cook 11 min-
utes, or until only a
small kernel of white
remains in the center.
Place in a colander and
rinse quickly with cold
water. Set aside or
refrigerate or freeze
until needed. When
ready to use, reheat the
rice in the microwave or
place in a colander, top
with a piece of wax
paper, and place over
hot water in a pan,
letting the water
steam it hot.

The orange and rosemary add a subtle, refreshing flavor to this very colorful, easy-to-prepare meal. Braising the meat and vegetables with very
little extra liquid intensifies the flavors. It is absolutely delicious!

2 tablespoons all-purpose flour
Grated peel (no white attached) of 2
    oranges
2 teaspoons paprika
2 teaspoons chopped fresh rosemary
Salt
Freshly ground black pepper
2 pounds boneless lamb shoulder,
    trimmed and cut into 1-inch pieces
2 tablespoons olive oil

4 carrots, cut into 3-inch julienne strips
½ cup dry white wine
½ cup fresh or canned chicken broth or
    stock
2 tablespoons fresh orange juice
1 cup fresh or frozen green peas
    (optional)
2 tablespoons chopped fresh parsley or
    mint
4 cups cooked white rice

In a plastic zip-type bag or in a bowl, combine the flour, orange peel, paprika, and rosemary. Season with salt and pepper. Add the lamb pieces and toss to
coat. In a large skillet over medium-high heat, heat the oil and add the dredged
lamb pieces, stirring until the meat is nicely browned on all sides, about 10 minutes. Add the carrots, wine, chicken stock, and orange juice and let the meat
braise, covered, 35 to 40 minutes, or until the lamb is tender. *The lamb can be
refrigerated for 3 or 4 days.* When ready to serve, bring back to the boil, add the
peas if using and herbs, and cook 5 minutes longer. Serve over the rice.

Serves 4 to 6

GRECIAN LAMB AND
EGGPLANT CASSEROLE

This casserole is delightful, with the bonus of being light in calories. Because eggplants can cook unattended, I'll often bake the eggplants one day (maybe doing some extra to freeze) and finish assembling and baking the casserole the next. The whole casserole may be made in advance and frozen, before or after baking. It freezes for up to 3 months.

2 large eggplants
2 tablespoons olive oil
1 medium onion, chopped
8 ounces lean ground lamb
1 28-ounce can Italian plum tomatoes,
   broken up with a spoon
½ teaspoon ground cinnamon
3 tablespoons fresh lemon juice
½ cup golden raisins

8 ounces pasta (bows, shells, fusilli, or
   the like), cooked and drained
1 cup nonfat or lowfat yogurt
1 teaspoon ground cumin
Salt
Freshly ground black pepper
1 cup fine dry breadcrumbs, tossed with 1
   to 2 tablespoons melted butter

Preheat the oven to 350°F. Grease a 9 × 12-inch casserole.

Cut the eggplants in half lengthwise and place, cut-side down, on a greased baking sheet. Place in the oven and bake 30 to 45 minutes, or until very tender. Alternatively, check microwave directions and microwave until soft and tender. Cool, then scrape the flesh from the skin of the eggplants into a bowl. *The cooked eggplant pulp can be refrigerated for several days*.

Heat the olive oil in a large skillet. Add the onion and cook until soft, 5 or 6 minutes. Add the lamb and cook until browned, breaking up with a wooden spoon, about 5 minutes. Pour off any excess grease. Add the tomatoes, cinnamon, 1 tablespoon of the lemon juice, and raisins. Bring to the boil, reduce the heat, and simmer 15 to 20 minutes, or until thickened.

Meanwhile, bring a large pot of salted water to the boil; add the pasta and cook just until al dente. Drain and set aside.

In a mixing bowl, combine the eggplant pulp, yogurt, cumin, salt and pepper to taste, and remaining lemon juice. Spread the eggplant mixture in the prepared casserole. Layer the pasta over the eggplant and top with the lamb-tomato mixture. Sprinkle with the breadcrumbs. **This can be done a couple of days in advance.** Bake 20 to 25 minutes, or until heated through. Serve hot.

Serves 4

LAMB WITH PRESERVED LEMONS

This unusual casserole is particularly delicious. It requires little attention from the cook, lending itself to the kind of meal one puts on before running errands or doing the laundry, then "eats on" all week. The addition of fresh peas makes cooking a separate green vegetable unnecessary. It may be prepared in stages, or completed and kept refrigerated or frozen. It freezes for up to 6 months.

3 pounds boneless lamb shoulder
1 tablespoon finely chopped fresh ginger
¾ teaspoon crumbled saffron
2 tablespoons butter
½ tablespoon salt

2 cups shelled fresh or frozen peas
1 preserved lemon peel (page 158),
  finely chopped
12 green olives, preferably Greek, brine
  packed

Cut the lamb into 2½- to 3-inch pieces and put it in a large, heavy oven-proof casserole. Add the ginger, saffron, butter, salt, and enough water to cover. Bring to the boil, reduce the heat, and simmer, covered, stirring occasionally, until the meat is meltingly tender (about 1 to 1½ hours). **The lamb can be pre-pared to this point and refrigerated for several days.**

Return the stew to a simmer. Add the peas to the casserole, plus additional water if needed to cover, and simmer 3 to 5 minutes. When the peas are near-ly cooked, add the preserved lemon peel and olives. Bring to the boil, lower the heat, and simmer until the sauce is syrupy, about 3 minutes, taking care not to overcook the peas. Serve hot with orzo or couscous.

Serves 6 to 8

LAMB AND ITALIAN SAUSAGE STEW

Ray and I created this dish in early May on a chilly, dreary day, the kind just perfect for a fire in the fireplace but a little late in the year to have one. We went with our feelings rather than the calendar and enjoyed this delicious stew, warming ourselves by the crackling fire, savoring the last one of the season. I've made this stew with the meat in large pieces, still attached to the shoulder blade, as well as with boneless cubes. I think there is more flavor in the bone-in meat, but of course the stew is easier to eat without the bones. It's particularly delicious because the beans are cooked with the meat juices. If you really don't have time to cook it this long, you may precook the beans according to package directions, then add to the meats and cook the whole dish for an hour. It may be kept refrigerated up to 3 days, improving every day.

STEW SENSE
When preparing a slow-cooked dish like a stew, start cooking the longest thing—such as browning the meat—before slicing the vegetables. By the time the meat is nicely colored, the vegetables are ready to go in.

1 pound dried navy beans	1 bay leaf, crumbled
2 pounds Italian sausage, cut into 1½-inch pieces	1 tablespoon chopped fresh rosemary
	1 tablespoon chopped fresh oregano
4 pounds boneless lamb shoulder, cut into 1½-inch pieces	1 tablespoon chopped fresh thyme
	½ teaspoon red pepper flakes
3 onions, sliced	6 cups fresh or canned chicken stock or broth
2 garlic cloves, peeled and chopped	
2 cups sliced carrots	2 bunches spinach, washed and stemmed
1 28-ounce can whole tomatoes with juice, broken up	2 teaspoons poultry seasoning
	Salt
¼ cup red wine vinegar	Freshly ground black pepper

Wash the beans and place in a pot with water to cover. Bring to the boil, reduce the heat, cover, and simmer for 10 minutes. Remove from the heat and let sit 1 hour. Drain.

Meanwhile, in a large pan over medium-high heat, brown the sausage on all sides. Transfer the sausage to a side dish, reserving the fat in the pan. Add the lamb to the skillet and brown on all sides, taking care not to crowd the pan; you may need to brown the meat in 2 batches. Add the lamb to the browned sausages, reserving the fat. Add the onions, garlic, and carrots to the skillet and sauté until nicely browned, about 7 to 8 minutes.

In a large stockpot, combine the beans, sausage, lamb, onion mixture, tomatoes with their juice, vinegar, bay leaf, rosemary, oregano, thyme, and red pepper flakes. Add enough stock to cover. Bring to the boil slowly, skim off any scum, then reduce the heat and simmer, covered, for 2 to 2½ hours, or until the beans are tender. *The stew can be made to this point and refrigerated several days or frozen.*

When ready to serve, return the stew to the boil. Add the spinach, poultry seasoning, and salt and pepper to taste and cook 3 to 5 minutes more.

Serves 8

LAMB CHOPS WITH DIJON-ROSEMARY CRUST

Marinated ahead of time for maximum flavor, these chops are seared crisp on the outside with lean, pink, and juicy meat inside. This is a purely elegant entrée that is lovely presented with a sprig of fresh rosemary for each chop.

8 loin lamb chops, 1½ inches thick   2 tablespoons chopped fresh rosemary
½ cup Dijon mustard   ¼ cup red wine vinegar
3 garlic cloves, peeled and chopped   2 tablespoons cracked pepper
2 teaspoons chopped fresh ginger   Salt

Remove any excess fat from the chops. In a bowl, mix together the mustard, garlic, ginger, rosemary, vinegar, cracked pepper, and salt to taste. Rub on the chops and let marinate, refrigerated, for 4 to 6 hours or overnight.

Grill the chops 6 inches from the coals 4 to 5 minutes per side, or until a meat thermometer registers 140°F. for rare, 150°F. for medium.

Serves 4 to 6

VERSATILE LAMB STUFFING

This recipe will make enough stuffing to fill about 24 squash halves, 30 stuffed onion "leaves," or about 50 to 60 mushroom caps; the possibilities are endless. With the different variations, it will serve as an earthy entrée, a sensational side dish, or a very appealing appetizer. The choice is yours. It reheats very well, either on its own or stuffed in the vegetables. This can be frozen for 3 to 4 months.

3 tablespoons olive oil
2 pounds ground lamb or ground beef
1 onion, chopped
3 garlic cloves, peeled and chopped
1 eggplant, cut into ½-inch pieces
1 16-ounce can stewed tomatoes with
  juice
3 cups fresh or canned chicken stock
½ cup rice
2 tablespoons chopped fresh herbs (rosemary, basil, and/or oregano)
1 bay leaf, crumbled
2 teaspoons ground coriander

½ teaspoon ground cinnamon
¼ teaspoon mace
¼ to ½ teaspoon cayenne pepper
2 teaspoons paprika
Salt
Freshly ground black pepper
1 cup crumbled feta cheese
1 cup grated imported Parmesan cheese
12 zucchini or yellow squash or
  5 large onions or 50 to 60 large
  mushrooms
1 cup breadcrumbs (optional)

Preheat the oven to 375° F.

Heat the olive oil in a large ovenproof casserole. Add the ground meat, onion, garlic, and eggplant and sauté until the lamb is browned and the vegetables are soft, about 10 minutes. Drain off any excess grease. Add the stewed tomatoes, chicken stock, rice, fresh herbs, and bay leaf and cook, uncovered, until most of the liquid is absorbed, about 20 to 25 minutes. Stir in the coriander, cinnamon, mace, cayenne, paprika, and salt and pepper to taste. Stir in ½ cup of the feta cheese and ½ cup of the Parmesan. *The stuffing can be refrigerated for 3 or 4 days.*

For stuffed zucchini and yellow squash, slice the tips off the squash, then slice in half lengthwise. With a melon baller or spoon, hollow out the center and reserve the pulp for another use. Either microwave the shells in a shallow dish until soft enough to pierce with a fork but not mushy, about 3 to 5 minutes, or simmer them in water or chicken stock 5 to 7 minutes. Drain them, spoon in the filling, sprinkle with the remaining cheese and breadcrumbs if using, and bake 15 to 20 minutes, or until the tops are a lovely golden brown.

For stuffed onion "leaves," slice off the stem and root ends from the onion and peel it. Slice the onion down one side from the center to the outside edge. Place the onion in boiling water or chicken stock for about 5 minutes. Remove from the liquid and allow to cool. Separate the onion into its concentric layers. Place about 2 tablespoons of the filling in each layer, then roll them, and place them, seam-side down, in a baking dish. Sprinkle the rolls with the remaining cheese and breadcrumbs if using. Bake about 20 minutes, then broil for about 5 minutes, until golden brown.

For mushrooms, brush any excess dirt from the mushrooms. Remove the stems and save for stock. Brush each cap with butter or oil and fill with about 1 tablespoon of the filling. Sprinkle with the remaining cheese and breadcrumbs if using, and bake for about 20 minutes, until heated through.

Serves 6 to 8 as an entrée

CONVENIENCE CASSOULET

This recipe is a scaled-down version of the French classic, streamlined for speed and ease of preparation. You will be surprised at how closely it resembles the time-honored original in flavor, and the savings in time will make this the version of choice. It is the perfect large-group, low-cost party dish. Best of all, you can stop at virtually any point in the preparation and refrigerate the cassoulet for up to 2 days. It freezes for up to 2 months; defrost overnight in the refrigerator.

PREPARING DRIED BEANS
Dried lentils and beans are traditionally soaked overnight in enough water to cover by 2 inches. Or they can be brought to the boil, allowed to sit 1 hour, and then drained. You can omit this step and then cook for a longer time. It will add half an hour or so in the case of small lentils and an hour or so in the case of dried beans. Always be sure to check that you have enough liquid to allow them to soften completely and to cook without scorching (6 parts liquid to 1 part lentils or beans is usually safe).

2 pounds dried Great Northern beans
½ pound lean salt pork, blanched and
  drained, cut into ½-inch cubes
2 pounds pork loin or thick chops, cut
  into 1-inch cubes
2 pounds lamb chops, cut into 1-inch
  cubes
1½ pounds Polish kielbasa, cut into
  ½-inch slices
2 pounds boneless chicken, cut into
  ¾-inch cubes
3 large onions, chopped
8 garlic cloves, peeled and chopped
1 cup dry white wine

1 28-ounce can crushed tomatoes in
  tomato puree
1 28-ounce can whole plum tomatoes
  with juice, coarsely chopped
1 tablespoon poultry seasoning
1 tablespoon finely chopped fresh thyme
1 tablespoon finely chopped fresh basil
1 cup finely chopped fresh parsley
3 bay leaves, crumbled
Salt
Freshly ground black pepper
2 cups breadcrumbs
½ cup (1 stick) butter, melted

Pick over the beans and rinse well. Place in a large saucepan and cover with water, bring to the boil, cover, and simmer 10 minutes. Remove from the heat and let sit for 1 hour.

Place the salt pork in an 8-quart Dutch oven. Cook over medium heat, stirring occasionally, until the fat is rendered, 5 to 10 minutes. With a slotted spoon, remove the salt pork and reserve.

Add the pork and lamb and cook over high heat until well browned, about 8 minutes. Remove the pork and lamb, add the sausage and chicken, and cook until light brown all over, about 5 minutes. Remove the sausage and chicken from the pan. *The salt pork, lamb, pork, sausage, and chicken can be kept refrigerated a day or 2. Bring to room temperature before proceeding.* Set the browned meats aside.

Add the onions and garlic and cook until golden, about 7 to 8 minutes. Add the white wine, scraping the bottom and sides of the pan, and cook over high heat until reduced by half, 5 to 7 minutes. Return the salt pork, pork, lamb, sausage, and chicken to the pan. Add the crushed tomatoes, plum tomatoes, poultry seasoning, thyme, basil, parsley, bay leaves, and salt and plenty of pepper to taste. Drain the beans, reserving the liquid, and add the beans to the meat mixture, stirring well. Add enough of the bean liquid to just cover the beans. *At this point, the cassoulet can be covered and refrigerated for a day or 2.*

Preheat the oven to 325°F. Sprinkle the breadcrumbs on top, drizzle the melted butter over the cassoulet, and bake for 1 hour. After 1 hour, press the breadcrumbs down into the cassoulet. Add more of the reserved bean liquid if the cassoulet seems dry and return to the oven for 1 to 1½ hours, or until the beans are soft and tender.

Serves 16

HOME-STYLE HAM AND
POTATO CASSEROLE

This is comfort food at its best. The potatoes and onions, along with the ricotta cheese, form a wonderful gratin that emerges hot and bubbly from the oven. The addition of the country ham lends a down-home taste. Do not add salt; the cured ham provides all that is needed. This does not freeze, but it can be reheated and keeps 2 or 3 days in the refrigerator.

8 potatoes, peeled and thinly sliced	3 tablespoons chopped fresh rosemary
2 onions, thinly sliced	1 teaspoon black pepper
1 tablespoon olive oil	3 cups milk
1 pound country ham, thinly sliced	1 cup grated Swiss cheese
2 cups ricotta cheese	

Preheat the oven to 375°F.

In a large bowl, toss together the potatoes and onions and set aside. In a large skillet over medium heat, heat the oil and add the ham. Sauté the ham until just heated through, about 2 minutes. Remove from the pan and cut into thin strips. In a small bowl, mix together the ricotta cheese, rosemary, and black pepper. Place half of the potato-onion mixture in a 13 × 9 × 2-inch baking dish and top this with the ricotta cheese and ham strips. Cover with the remaining potatoes. Pour the milk over the entire casserole. Bake for 1½ hours, or until the potatoes are soft and the sauce is thick and bubbly. Top with the grated cheese and bake for 15 to 20 minutes more, or until the cheese melts.

Serves 6 to 9

PORK WITH ALMOND CRUST

BREADING
Breading is usually con-
sidered a last-minute
operation, but there are
real benefits to bread-
ing foods in advance.
Breading is used to pro-
tect delicate foods such
as fish fillets or veal
from the intense heat
of frying. The classic
method of breading is
to dredge the food in
flour, dip it in lightly
beaten egg, and then
coat it with bread-
crumbs. You can add
seasonings to the flour
or the breadcrumbs to
change the final flavor,
or use flour, cornmeal,
or biscuit crumbs in
place of the bread-
crumbs. Each con-
tributes a unique flavor
and texture. Once the
breading is applied, you
can refrigerate the
foods for a couple of
hours, and in fact
breading clings better
to food when it's
allowed to stand in the
fridge for an hour or
more. During this time,
the breading will dry
and will produce a
crisper crust. Some
foods, such as very deli-
cate croquettes, *must*
be refrigerated before
frying to ensure that
the center does not
overcook while the out-
side is getting properly
brown.

his delightful dish features tender, juicy pork with a crisp almond crust. It is a perfect make-ahead dish for entertaining. Breaded and refrigerated, the pork can be cooked in a snap, sautés quickly, and reheats beautifully in the microwave or a low oven, giving you time to enjoy your evening with friends. The pork retains its crunch and flavor for about 2 hours after cooking.

2 eggs
³⁄₄ cup buttermilk
³⁄₄ cup flour
³⁄₄ cup cracker crumbs
1 cup sliced almonds
1 teaspoon salt
¹⁄₂ teaspoon cayenne pepper
1 teaspoon ground coriander

6 pork loin cutlets, pounded ¹⁄₄ inch
   thick
Butter
Olive oil

GARNISH
3 green onions, sliced
Lemon wedges

In a small bowl, mix together the eggs and buttermilk. In another bowl, combine the flour, cracker crumbs, almonds, salt, cayenne pepper, and coriander. Dip the pounded cutlets into the egg mixture, then dredge them in the flour mixture, pressing the breading on to make the almonds adhere. Lay the cutlets on a baking sheet and refrigerate for at least 1 hour. *This can be done up to 24 hours in advance.* When ready to serve, heat enough butter and olive oil to cover the bottom of a large skillet until "singing" hot. Cook the cutlets 3 at a time, turning and cooking about 3 to 4 minutes per side, or until the almonds are golden and browned. Drain on paper towels. Sprinkle with the sliced green onions and accompany with the lemon wedges.

Serves 6

BARBECUED PORK LOIN

This super easy marinated loin can be cooked just before serving. The all-purpose marinade can be kept refrigerated for several weeks, just waiting for thinly sliced pork loin or even chicken breasts to flavor. Save half the marinade for another time if you're cooking just a few pieces of meat, or double it (and the salsa) to feed a crowd. The pork is best served with salsa, which can be made ahead, and keeps several days, refrigerated. The pork does not freeze well and is only so-so reheated, but by having everything done ahead except the last-minute grilling you maximize the flavor and the use of your time.

PORK LOIN
Boned pork loin is a large piece of meat about 24 inches long. It may be cut into smaller, individual roasts or folded in half for a large roast that is good eating for several days. Since the meat is cooked according to thickness, you can control the cooking time by doubling the loin in half or by cooking it in a single layer, depending on your needs.

1 tablespoon vegetable oil
1 small onion, chopped
1 cup ketchup
⅓ cup vinegar
2 tablespoons packed brown sugar
  (light or dark)
½ cup Worcestershire sauce
1 tablespoon prepared mustard

½ cup soy sauce
Salt
Freshly ground black pepper
8 slices boneless pork loin, cut ½ inch
  thick

Black Bean and Corn Salsa (page 155)

In a small saucepan, heat the oil. Add the onion and cook over moderately low heat until soft, 5 or 6 minutes. Add the ketchup, vinegar, brown sugar, Worcestershire, mustard, soy sauce, and salt and pepper to taste, and bring to the boil over medium heat. Turn off the heat and cool to room temperature. *This keeps several weeks in the refrigerator in a tightly covered jar.*

Place the pork slices in a shallow pan and cover with the marinade. Marinate at least 1 to 2 hours and as long as 3 days.

Preheat the grill or broiler. Remove the pork from the sauce and place on the hot grill or on a greased pan under the broiler. Cook approximately 4 to 5 minutes per side, or until just done. Serve hot or at room temperature, with Black Bean and Corn Salsa.

Serves 4

HOISIN AND HONEY PORK LOIN

Dishes like this one that are prepared over the course of three days—marinating one day, cooking the next, slicing the third—are ideal for busy schedules. The marinade gives this loin a deep, rich flavor, even when sliced thinly for a buffet, and it makes great sandwiches.

MARINADE
1 7-ounce jar hoisin sauce
½ cup honey
¼ cup soy sauce
¼ cup rice wine vinegar
1 tablespoon chopped fresh ginger

3 garlic cloves, peeled and chopped
6 to 8 green onions, chopped
1 tablespoon sesame seeds
¼ to ½ teaspoon red pepper flakes

1 5- to 6-pound boned pork loin

In a large bowl, combine the hoisin sauce, honey, soy sauce, rice wine vinegar, ginger, garlic, green onions, sesame seeds, and red pepper flakes. Pour over the pork loin and marinate in the refrigerator for 2 hours and up to 24 hours.

Preheat the oven to 350°F.

Remove the loin from the marinade, reserving the marinade, and fold the meat in half lengthwise, tying it with kitchen twine in 2 or 3 places. Place in a roasting pan and cook for about 2 to 2½ hours, or until a meat thermometer registers 150°F. You may need to tent the meat with foil if it starts to burn. Remove from the oven, cut the string, and let the pork loin sit for 10 minutes before slicing. **The pork can be refrigerated for 24 hours.** Arrange the slices on a platter. Meanwhile, put the reserved marinade in a saucepan, bring to the boil, then reduce the heat and simmer for 10 minutes, or until the sauce has thickened. Pour some over the sliced pork and pass the rest separately.

Serves 6 to 8

PORK LOIN WITH SPICED PEACH CHUTNEY

Savory peach chutney gives roasted pork a lift. Frozen peaches may be used for the chutney, but fresh ripe and juicy ones are superior. The chutney will keep 2 to 3 weeks in the refrigerator, so it certainly can be made in advance, though it won't have the flavor of the pork drippings.

1 tablespoon olive oil
1 3-pound pork loin (½ of a large loin)

CHUTNEY
4 peaches, peeled and sliced, or 1 pound frozen
2 garlic cloves, peeled and chopped
1 small onion, chopped
2 green onions, green part only, chopped
1 tablespoon chopped fresh ginger
½ cup apple cider vinegar

¼ cup packed brown sugar (light or dark)
3 tablespoons fresh lemon juice
½ cup raisins or currants
2 teaspoons Dijon mustard
1 teaspoon mustard seeds
¼ teaspoon cayenne pepper (optional)
Salt
Freshly ground black pepper
¼ cup toasted slivered almonds

Preheat the oven to 350°F.

In a large skillet, heat the oil over medium-high heat. Add the loin and brown on all sides for about 8 to 10 minutes. Transfer the meat to a roasting pan and bake 45 minutes in the oven, or until a meat thermometer registers 150°F. Set aside.

Meanwhile, in the skillet you browned the meat in, combine the peaches, garlic, onion, green onions, ginger, vinegar, brown sugar, lemon juice, raisins, mustard, mustard seeds, cayenne pepper if using, and salt and pepper to taste. Cook until thick and most of the liquid has cooked out, about 20 minutes. Cool and pour into 1 or 2 tightly covered jars or set aside at room temperature.

To serve, slice the loin and arrange the slices on a large platter. Pour the chutney over the loin and serve hot or at room temperature. Garnish with slivered almonds if desired.

Serves 6 to 8

ROOT VEGETABLES WITH PORK TENDERLOIN

MAKING STEWS AHEAD
Since most stews are better made ahead, I usually make 2 or 3 batches at a time. I cut up and cook all the onions and garlic at one time. Then I brown the meat for several recipes. This means I only have one greasy cleanup instead of several. When I have time, later that day or the next, I finish cooking all of the stew. Then I store the extra in the refrigerator or wrap and freeze it for later. This way, I reduce my work load and clean-up considerably.

There are many possible stopping points in this recipe. It can be fixed all at once, or the vegetables can be cooked ahead of time and combined with the pork 1 hour before serving time. In addition, the whole dish reheats in the microwave or 350°F. oven. It is a hearty, tasty meal that gives a real feeling of abundance and will satisfy the meat-and-potatoes man who is also watching how much meat he eats. It may be made 1 to 2 days in advance.

1 to 2 tablespoons olive oil
2 medium onions, cut into 1-inch cubes
3 medium turnips, peeled and cut into 1-inch cubes
3 medium sweet potatoes, peeled and cut into 1-inch cubes
1 cup fresh or canned chicken stock or broth
2 pork tenderloins (1 pound each)

R U B
3 to 4 teaspoons chopped fresh ginger
1 tablespoon soy sauce
2 garlic cloves, peeled and chopped
¼ teaspoon Chinese five-spice powder
   (available at Oriental groceries)

Salt
Freshly ground black pepper

Preheat the oven to 350°F.

In a large frying pan, heat 1 tablespoon of the olive oil. Add the onions and sauté until soft, 5 to 7 minutes. Remove the onions to a 9 × 13-inch casserole, reserving the fat in the pan. Add the turnips, sweet potatoes, and chicken broth to the casserole. *This can be done up to 4 hours in advance.*

Meanwhile, rub the pork with ginger, soy sauce, garlic, and five-spice powder. Place in the hot frying pan with more oil if necessary. Brown, turn, and brown all over, 8 to 10 minutes. Remove the tenderloins from the pan and place them on top of the vegetables. Season to taste with salt and pepper. *The recipe can be made an hour or 2 ahead to this point.* Bake 30 to 40 minutes, or until the pork reaches an internal temperature of 160°F. Remove the tenderloins and keep warm. Stir the vegetables and bake another 10 to 15 minutes, or until tender. Slice the meat and mix with the vegetables. Serve hot.

Serves 4 to 6

FRESH PORK ROAST WITH DRIED FRUIT

The shank portion of a fresh leg of pork, technically the ham, is a very tender piece of meat. Dried fruit enhances the meat, adding a lovely sweetness. This roast is one of my favorites for a dinner party or a cocktail buffet because it feeds so many people with so little effort. The meat reheats very well, so it may be made several days in advance, and any leftovers will be relished.

1 9- to 10-pound fresh pork ham, shank
  portion
4½ cups fresh or canned chicken stock or
  broth
1 cup dried cherries
1 cup dried apricots

1 cup dried currants
2 to 3 tablespoons flour
2 tablespoons water
Salt
Freshly ground black pepper

Preheat the oven to 400° F.

Place the pork in a large roasting pan and bake, uncovered, for 1½ hours. Reduce the heat to 375° F. and continue cooking for ½ hour. Add 2½ cups stock to the pan and cook another ½ hour. Now add the dried fruit to the pan and continue cooking until the pork reaches an internal temperature of 160° F., about 15 minutes to ½ hour.

Transfer the meat to a carving board and set aside. Pour the pan juices through a strainer, reserving the fruit and cooking liquid separately. Skim off the fat. ***The roast can be prepared to this point a day in advance.***

Place the liquid and remaining 2 cups of stock in a saucepan and bring to the boil. Stir the flour and water together in a small bowl until smooth, then whisk into the stock mixture and simmer until thickened, about 5 minutes. Return the fruit to the sauce and season with salt and pepper. Slice the roast and serve hot or at room temperature passing the sauce separately.

Serves 8 to 10

Roasted Cornish Hens with Shallots ■ Pesto-Stuffed Cornish Hens
with Pasta ■ Peppery Cornish Hens with Mixed Fresh Vegetables
■ Chicken in a Pot ■ Copper Chicken ■ Slow Slow Chicken ■
Tex-Mex Roast Chicken ■ Curried Roast Chicken with Potatoes
and Apples ■ Chicken Couscous with Harissa ■ Indian-Style
Chicken ■ Jamaican Jerked Chicken ■ Chicken Thighs in a Honey-
Sesame Marinade ■ Pierre-Henri's Lemon Chicken ■ Deviled

P O U L T R Y & F I S H

Chicken ■ Duck with Orange and Mint ■ Oriental Turkey Loaf ■
Turkey Breast Pistou ■ Turkey Croquettes ■ Turkey Tonnato ■
Baked Herbed Fish Fillets ■ Baked or Microwaved Fillets of
Flounder with Moroccan Spices ■ Salad of Poached Fish with
Grapes ■ Baked Moroccan Swordfish Steaks with Lemons and
Onion Confit ■ Smoked Trout ■ Salmon with Tomato-Cream
Sauce ■ Shrimp with Spicy Peanut Sauce or Dip ■ Gravlax

PEOPLE TEND TO associate chicken with last-minute stir fries or sautés, but it takes beautifully to stewing, marinating, and, of course, roasting. I am never without a whole chicken in my freezer. I open the whole chicken, remove the inner package of gizzards and liver, and rewrap the chicken before freezing. I can defrost it either in the microwave or overnight in the refrigerator. It's then ready to be thrown in the oven with little ado for a spectacular Copper Chicken or to be cut up and tossed into the pot for Pierre-Henri's Lemon Chicken. Either way, the chicken cooks virtually unattended while I whip up a dessert and get the vegetables done, with truly satisfying results.

I also bone and freeze chicken breasts, making a stock from the bones, which also gets put into the freezer for another time. (Of course you can buy boneless breasts, but they're more expensive and don't yield the bonus of homemade stock.) I freeze the chicken breasts flat, separately, then wrap them in plastic for quick defrosting and cooking.

The grill is particularly kind to chicken breasts. If I can get a helper to start the coals, I'm thrilled! When time is short, I use my stovetop grill or the broiler and am perfectly satisfied. I do try to plan ahead, doing my defrosting and marinating a day ahead whenever possible to increase flavor with little effort.

I find that one-pot dishes like Chicken Couscous with Harissa, where I can cook everything together, take less time in the long run than individual vegetables and entrées. Cornish hens are another standby. They make an elegant dinner in no time.

Fish, too, has become a very important part of my diet. It is not just its low fat content, although that helps my waistline and my health; it is also its ease of cooking and its accommodation to a variety of ingredients. The flavor and texture of a fish can be completely different depending on whether it's grilled, poached, baked, served with curried apples, baked with garlic and vinegar, served with Asian, Mexican, or Moroccan ingredients.

Fish is one of the hardest things to cook unattended. By its very composition it lends itself to fast cooking and you are at its beck and call. And I'm rarely thrilled with reheated fish. It tends to overcook easily, resulting in a tough, unappetizing dish. (Fortunately, cold fish is good in salads or with pasta.) There are several ways to gain some time control over fish, however. One is increasing its thickness. The Canadian rule of thumb for cooking fish is to cook it ten minutes for each inch of thickness at 400°F. or more. I've found if I cook fish on a bed of ingredients, as in Salmon with Tomato-Cream Sauce, it extends the time it takes to cook. Whole fish and fish steaks cook longer than fish fillets of the same variety. Smoking fish is a much slower process and gives a bit of control. I cultivate recipes where everything can be assembled ahead of time, with only the final heating/cooking done at meal time, while I set the table and finish a few other odds and ends. Cold fish salads and dishes where the fish is marinated or dry rubbed also create ease of final preparation. And, finally, cured fish takes "little people" time, as it can be made over several days.

ROASTED CORNISH HENS
WITH SHALLOTS

Cornish hens are the answer to my prayers when I'm short of "people time." They cook so well unattended that I can get the rest of the dinner organized and still feel fresh when it's time to eat! Shallots, those tiny root vegetables that outdo onions for flavor per inch, enhance the birds magically; I love them cooked in butter and seasoned with a hint of rosemary. Cornish hens can serve 1 or 2 people each, depending on the appetites of the eaters and the side dishes provided. Leftovers reheat well and are good cold.

4 sprigs of rosemary
4 Cornish hens with their giblets and
  neck bones

6 tablespoons butter or oil
20 to 30 shallots, peeled (see Note)

Preheat the oven to 400°F.

Place a sprig of rosemary in the cavity of each bird. Rub the skins of each bird with the butter or oil and tie their legs together. Place the hens in a baking pan and surround with the peeled shallots. *The trussed birds can be refrigerated for 3 or 4 hours, well wrapped. Bring to room temperature before cooking.*

Bake the hens 45 minutes to 1 hour, turning once after about ½ hour when brown on one side. Remove the hens and shallots from the oven when the hens have reached a temperature of 180°F. on a meat thermometer and are brown all over. Cover loosely with foil and keep warm. Bring the pan juices to the boil and boil over medium-high heat until slightly thick. Cut down the backbone and place half a hen on each plate. Surround with some shallots. Spoon some sauce over the Cornish hens. Arrange the extra hens and shallots on a platter, garnished with rosemary.

Serves 4

N O T E : *To peel shallots with ease, half fill a frying pan with oil and heat to 350°F. Add the shallots and cook 1 to 2 minutes. Remove one with a slotted spoon or strainer. Rub with a towel. If it peels easily, remove the rest. Save the oil for another purpose.*

CARING FOR POULTRY
Much of the poultry available in supermarkets is now sold chilled to just above freezing. If properly cared for, it can be frozen, defrosted, and refrozen without making anyone ill, but you will sacrifice some flavor and juiciness, so a refrozen chicken should be used in casseroles or soups whenever possible. To care for store-bought poultry remove it from its packaging well before the expiration date. Remove the giblets and neck, if any, from the cavity. Wrap loosely in plastic wrap, foil, or a plastic bag and store in the refrigerator up to 3 days. If not used, freeze, tightly sealed, for 3 months.

Salmonella is killed by heat and is usually found only on the surface area of poultry. Always cook to an internal temperature of 180°F.

I don't advocate rinsing poultry before using it unless boiling water is used. Anything less simply spreads any bacteria that might exist.

PESTO-STUFFED CORNISH
HENS WITH PASTA

This lovely dish is simple but perfect for company. I usually serve half a
bird per person, but if you want an abundance, allow one per person.
Be sure to use a small roasting pan, as the lovely juices may evaporate in a
large one.

2 Cornish hens (1½ to 2 pounds each)   *½ pound angel hair pasta*
⅔ cup Pesto Sauce (page 155)

Preheat the oven to 400°F.

Loosen the skin of the hens with your fingers. Use a small spoon or your
fingers to place about ¼ cup of pesto between the meat and loosened skin.
Tie the legs together and fold the wings under to give the birds a nice shape
and to hold the skin together. *The trussed birds can be refrigerated 3 to 4 hours
or overnight, well wrapped. Bring to room temperature before cooking.* Place
the hens in a small roasting pan and bake 30 to 45 minutes, basting once or
twice, until the juices run clear and the birds are well browned. Remove the
birds, set aside, cover loosely with foil, and keep warm.

Bring the pan juices to the boil over high heat and boil until slightly thickened, about 5 minutes.

Cook the pasta in boiling salted water by package directions, about 2 to
3 minutes for fresh. Drain well and toss the pasta with the reduced pan
juices and 3 tablespoons pesto sauce. Place the pasta on a platter and top with
the birds.

Serves 2 to 4

PEPPERY CORNISH HENS WITH MIXED FRESH VEGETABLES

I love easy one-dish meals. This one is especially easy when the hens are marinated and the vegetables are sliced the day before and kept covered in the refrigerator. You can substitute 4 to 6 chicken breasts for the Cornish hens. Reduce the baking time accordingly.

2 Cornish game hens

Grated peel (no white attached) of 3
  lemons

1/4 cup fresh lemon juice

1/2 cup chopped green onions

2 tablespoons coarsely ground black
  pepper

1 tablespoon brown sugar (light or dark)

1 teaspoon salt

6 zucchini, sliced

2 red onions, halved and sliced

2 red bell peppers, seeded and sliced

1 cup long-grain rice

2 tablespoons chopped fresh thyme

2 tablespoons chopped fresh parsley

2 3/4 cups fresh or canned chicken stock or
  broth

Salt

Freshly ground black pepper

Preheat the oven to 400°F.

With poultry shears, cut down each side of the Cornish hens' backbones and discard the backbone. Turn the bird over, and with the heel of your hand, press on the breastbone to flatten. Set aside.

In a medium-size bowl, toss together the lemon peel, lemon juice, green onions, pepper, brown sugar, and salt. Place the birds in the bowl, turning several times to coat evenly. Set aside to marinate up to 3 hours while preparing the vegetables. In a large bowl, mix together the zucchini slices, red onions, red peppers, rice, thyme, parsley, and chicken stock, and season to taste with salt and pepper. Pour into a lightly oiled 13 × 9-inch baking dish, top with the Cornish hens, pouring any reserved marinade over the vegetables. Bake 50 to 60 minutes, or until the hens register 180°F. on a meat thermometer and the rice is tender.

Serves 4

CHICKEN IN A POT

Here is a comforting one-dish meal that takes very little time to put together and cooks on its own. You needn't peel the potatoes and carrots unless you prefer to for aesthetic reasons, and you certainly can substitute water for the chicken broth, although the stock won't be as rich. This can be made ahead a couple of days or frozen. It freezes for up to 3 months if you omit the potatoes when cooking.

1 3½-pound chicken
1 onion, cut into chunks
2 garlic cloves, peeled and chopped
4 carrots, scrubbed and cut into 1-inch chunks
4 celery stalks, chopped
4 medium potatoes, scrubbed and quartered
1 bay leaf, crumbled

1 tablespoon finely chopped fresh thyme or 1 teaspoon dried (optional)
1 tablespoon finely chopped fresh parsley (optional)
Salt
Freshly ground black pepper
2 cups fresh or canned chicken stock or broth or water

Preheat the oven to 375°F.

In a large Dutch oven, place the chicken, onion, garlic, carrots, celery, potatoes, bay leaf, thyme, and parsley if using. Season to taste with salt and pepper. Pour the chicken stock or water around the chicken, cover, and bake 1 hour. Remove the cover and bake 30 minutes longer, or until a meat thermometer inserted in the thigh measures 180°F. and the vegetables are tender.

Serves 4 to 6

N O T E : *This recipe may be adapted for roasting bag use. Shake 2 tablespoons of flour in a large roasting bag and place in a roasting pan. Put vegetables and spices in the bottom of the bag and top with the chicken; do not add any additional liquid. Seal the bag and make 6 slits in the top. Cook in a preheated 325°F. oven for 2½ hours.*

COPPER CHICKEN

Roast chicken is one of the easiest and most adaptable main dishes there is. While the chicken is roasting, cook a starch, blanch a green vegetable (page 128), set the table, and you'll still have half an hour to make a salad or take a hot bath. This recipe is a variation on the classic roast chicken. Its copper color comes from paprika that's rubbed into the skin. I love the chicken stuffed with orange and garlic cloves, but if you are in a hurry the garlic can be cooked ahead, the orange omitted, and you'll still have a fabulous meal. This dish is good cold as well as hot, is wonderful on a picnic, and reheats well (although the skin is not as crisp), when frozen or made ahead a day or two.

½ teaspoon salt

½ to 1 teaspoon freshly ground black pepper

1 tablespoon plus ½ teaspoon paprika

1 5- to 6-pound roasting chicken

2 tablespoons melted butter or vegetable oil

2 heads garlic (about 24 cloves), peeled

Grated peel (no white attached) of 1 orange

2 bay leaves

2 sprigs of fresh rosemary

3 to 4 cups fresh or canned chicken stock or broth

1 tablespoon chopped fresh rosemary

Freshly ground black pepper

Preheat the oven to 400°F.

In a bowl, combine the salt, pepper, and 1 tablespoon of the paprika. Rub the chicken with the butter or oil and then with the spice mixture. Stuff the cavity of the bird with the garlic cloves, half of the orange peel, bay leaves, and rosemary sprigs. Truss the legs and place the chicken in a large baking dish. *The trussed chicken can be refrigerated for 3 or 4 hours, well wrapped. Bring to room temperature before cooking.*

Add enough stock to come 1 inch up the side of the chicken. Place in the oven and bake 1 to 1½ hours, or until a meat thermometer inserted in the thigh registers 180°F. Transfer the chicken to a cutting board and let sit 10 minutes before carving.

Add any remaining stock to the pan and bring to the boil over medium-high heat, stirring and scraping the cooked bits from the bottom of the pan. Add the remaining orange peel, chopped rosemary, and ½ teaspoon paprika; season to taste with salt and pepper. Continue to boil until the sauce is reduced by about one-third, about 5 to 10 minutes.

Arrange the carved chicken on a serving platter and pass a bowl of the sauce separately.

Serves 4 to 6

ROASTING BAGS
These specially constructed bags seem perfect for the busy cook. They make the process of cleanup enormously easier and provide brown yet moist foods that cook virtually unattended. Always follow package directions, which generally incude dusting at least 1 tablespoon of flour in the bag before adding the rest of the ingredients, slashing the bag 6 times, and maintaining an oven temperature of less than 400° F. Since the low heat (I usually cook at 325° F.) and long cooking (the average 2½- to 3-pound chuck roast or chicken plus a bed of vegetables takes about 2½ hours to cook) produce 2 to 3 cups liquid, I either reduce the liquid and serve it as a sauce or pour out enough liquid to cook couscous or rice, which lends it extraordinary flavor.

SLOW SLOW CHICKEN

This is an easy, easy way to cook chicken. Just pop it in a roasting bag and come back in 2½ hours. Moist, tender, and brown—it is absolutely delicious.

2 tablespoons all-purpose flour
1 onion, sliced
1 3-pound roasting chicken

Fresh thyme, oregano, or marjoram
(optional)

Preheat the oven to 325° F.

Shake the flour into a roasting bag. Put half the onion in the cavity of the chicken. Place the bag on a roasting pan, then add the rest of the onion. Place the chicken on top. Put some of the fresh herbs if using in the cavity of the chicken and sprinkle the rest over the chicken. Place the chicken in the roasting bag and close according to package directions and slit the bag in 6 places. Place in the oven and cook 2½ hours, or until a thermometer registers 180° F. Carefully open the bag. Remove the chicken and onions. Pour the liquid into a saucepan and discard the bag. Bring the liquid to the boil and reduce (see sidebar, page 114) until saucelike.

Serves 4 to 6

TEX-MEX ROAST CHICKEN

A very easy marinade makes this tangy, limey chicken dish a winner. Sprinkle with chopped fresh cilantro if desired.

MARINADE
½ cup fresh lime juice
½ to 1 cup fresh or canned chicken stock
  or broth
¼ cup red wine vinegar
4 garlic cloves, peeled and chopped
6 green onions, chopped
1 tablespoon chili powder
1 teaspoon ground cumin
1 teaspoon cumin seeds

¼ to ½ teaspoon cayenne pepper or 1
  jalapeño pepper, chopped
¼ cup chopped cilantro
Grated peel (no white attached) of 2
  limes
Salt
Freshly ground black pepper

1 3½-pound chicken, patted dry

In a medium-size bowl, mix together the lime juice, ½ cup of chicken stock, red wine vinegar, garlic, green onions, chili powder, ground cumin, cumin seeds, cayenne or jalapeño pepper, cilantro, and lime peel. Season to taste with salt and pepper. Place the chicken in a large bowl or resealable plastic bag and cover with the marinade. Marinate at least 1 hour and up to 24 hours in the refrigerator.

Preheat the oven to 400°F. Place the marinated chicken together with the marinade in a roasting pan. Add more stock if needed to come 1 inch up the side of the chicken. Bake, basting every 20 minutes, for 1 to 1¼ hours, or until a meat thermometer registers 180°F. when inserted into the thigh.

Serves 4

NOTE: *For a nice sauce, degrease the pan juices, then simmer 10 minutes with a tablespoon of cornstarch dissolved in a tablespoon of water.*

CURRIED ROAST CHICKEN
WITH POTATOES AND APPLES

**HANDY
CHICKEN**
Anytime you roast or
poach a whole chicken,
cook a second chicken
along with your recipe.
When cooked, remove
the meat from the bone
to use in the next day
or so, or freeze. Four to
six ounces of boneless
chicken per person is
about right. With the
bone, figure ¾ pound
per person. Use for
chicken soup, in salads,
or in rice casseroles.

This is a fast, one-pot meal bursting with flavor from the curry and cinnamon and made refreshingly aromatic by the orange rind. The vegetables simmer in the lovely juices, adding their own special richness to the
broth, which is delightful served with a crusty French bread to mop up all the
goodness.

3 tablespoons curry powder, preferably
    Madras
1 tablespoon paprika
½ teaspoon red pepper
½ teaspoon ground cardamom
½ teaspoon cinnamon
Salt
Freshly ground black pepper
1 3½-pound chicken, patted dry
2 sweet potatoes, peeled and cut into
    1-inch chunks

2 baking potatoes, cut into 1-inch chunks
2 onions, cut into eighths
2 tart apples, cored and cut into 1-inch
    chunks
1 orange, juiced (reserve the orange
    halves)
½ cup white wine
½ cup fresh or canned chicken stock or
    broth

Preheat the oven to 400°F.

In a small bowl, mix together the curry powder, paprika, red pepper, cardamom, and cinnamon. Season to taste with salt and pepper. Rub over the
entire chicken, sprinkling any excess into the cavity. Place the chicken in a
large roasting pan and surround with the sweet potatoes, baking potatoes,
onions, and apples. *This can be done an hour or 2 in advance and refrigerated.*
Mix together the orange juice (put the shells into the chicken cavity for extra
flavor), the wine, and the chicken stock. Pour over the vegetables. Bake the
chicken 1 to 1¼ hours, covering with foil after 45 minutes if the skin begins to
brown too quickly. The chicken is done when a meat thermometer inserted
into the thigh registers 180°F. and when the juices run clear when pierced
with a fork.

Serves 4 to 6

CHICKEN COUSCOUS
WITH HARISSA

The vegetables steal the show in this dish, with the chicken playing a supporting role, and despite the low calories, it's amazingly satisfying. I get all the vegetables cut up while I'm browning the chicken. It doesn't distract me from my other chores to go back twice and add them as the chicken cooks.

The harissa, a hot pepper sauce, is added at the table so everyone can determine the appropriate degree of spiciness for themselves. The sweet potatoes in this dish don't freeze well, but if you substitute carrots for the potatoes, it will freeze for 2 to 3 months with no problems. It reheats well either way.

1 to 2 tablespoons olive oil	3 yellow squash, cut into 1-inch cubes
1 3½-pound chicken, cut into serving pieces	2 zucchini, cut into 1-inch cubes
3 medium onions, cut into 1-inch cubes	HARISSA
2 teaspoons salt	¼ cup tomato paste
¼ teaspoon cayenne pepper	2 teaspoons cayenne pepper
½ teaspoon turmeric	1 teaspoon ground cumin
2 tablespoons tomato paste	1 teaspoon ground coriander
4 to 6 cups fresh or canned chicken stock or broth or water	Pinch of salt
	2 tablespoons olive oil
2 medium sweet potatoes, peeled and cut into 1-inch cubes	4 cups cooked couscous

Heat the oil in a large sauté pan. Add the chicken, skin-side down, and brown on both sides, about 15 minutes total. Remove to a side dish. Add the onions to the fat in the pan and cook until softened, 5 to 7 minutes. Stir in the salt, cayenne, and turmeric, then return the chicken to the pan and add the tomato paste and enough stock to cover. Bring to the boil, reduce the heat, and simmer, covered, for 30 minutes. Add the potatoes and cook for 15 minutes. Add the squash and zucchini and cook 15 minutes longer, or until the vegetables are soft, adding more stock if necessary. Remove the meat and vegetables with a slotted spoon. Skim the fat from the sauce, bring to the boil, and boil until reduced by about half, about 10 minutes.

Meanwhile, make the harissa. In a small bowl, combine the tomato paste, cayenne, cumin, coriander, salt, olive oil, and 2 tablespoons of the chicken cooking liquid. Whisk until well blended. *This can be done several days in advance and stored, tightly covered, in the refrigerator.*

Mound the couscous in the center of a very large platter. Surround with the meat and vegetables. Pass the sauce and the harissa separately.

Serves 4

INDIAN-STYLE CHICKEN

This crisp, succulent, spicy, and moist chicken is very similar to the Indian food I ate when I lived in London, which is perhaps the best place to eat it outside of India. If you want yours fire-eater hot, just up the cayenne.

¼ cup vegetable oil	*1 teaspoon ground ginger*
1 medium onion, chopped	*2 teaspoons paprika*
2 tablespoons ground coriander	*½ teaspoon cayenne pepper*
2 tablespoons turmeric	*2 cups plain yogurt*
1 tablespoon ground cardamom	*6 to 8 chicken breasts on the bone*

Heat the oil in a large saucepan. Add the onion and cook 2 to 3 minutes, or until the onion just starts to soften. Add the coriander, turmeric, cardamom, ginger, paprika, and cayenne and continue to cook for 3 to 5 minutes longer. Remove the mixture to a large mixing bowl, cool slightly, and stir in the yogurt until well combined. Add the chicken breasts and marinate 1 to 2 hours or overnight.

Preheat the oven to 350°F. Remove the chicken from the marinade and place on a baking sheet, preferably nonstick. Bake 45 to 50 minutes, or just until done.

Serves 6 to 8

JAMAICAN JERKED CHICKEN

A reflection of the Jamaican predilection for meat doused with hot chili sauce, this Jamaican chicken is traditionally grilled in charcoal pits and usually calls for lots of fiery-hot Scotch bonnet peppers. My palate can't tolerate that much heat, so I generally reduce the amount of peppers or substitute a milder variety. Aficionados with cast-iron tongues can always add more peppers. I oven bake it for ease, but grilling is traditional. This does not freeze well, but it can be reheated in the microwave and is good at room temperature as well as hot.

JERK SEASONING
2 teaspoons ground allspice
¼ teaspoon freshly grated nutmeg
½ tablespoon ground coriander
6 garlic cloves, peeled and chopped
2 tablespoons chopped fresh ginger
1 teaspoon ground cinnamon
1 Scotch bonnet, serrano, or jalapeño
  chile pepper, seeded and chopped

4 scallions or green onions, chopped
2 to 3 tablespoons olive oil
4 tablespoons lime juice

1 3½-pound broiler-fryer, cut into 8
  pieces

Place the allspice, nutmeg, ground coriander, garlic, ginger, cinnamon, hot pepper, scallions, olive oil, and 2 tablespoons lime juice in a food processor or blender and process until it forms a smooth paste. Rub all surfaces of the chicken with the spice mixture, lifting the skin and placing some under the skin. Refrigerate, covered, 8 hours or overnight.

Preheat the oven to 400°F.

Arrange the chicken on a broiler pan and bake for 35 minutes. Increase the oven temperature to broil, sprinkle the chicken with the remaining 2 tablespoons lime juice, and broil 4 to 5 minutes, or until lightly crisped.

Serves 4 to 6

CHICKEN THIGHS IN A
HONEY-SESAME MARINADE

MARINATING
Historically, a marinade
is a seasoned liquid in
which meat, fish, poul-
try, game, or vegetables
are soaked to flavor or
to tenderize somewhat.
Lately, dry mixtures of
ground herbs and/or
spices have come on
the scene to add flavor
to dishes. These dry
rubs are technically not
marinades, I suppose,
but they do enhance the
flavor and benefit from
a long exposure time.
    The time required to
marinate a given food
depends on its density
and how it has been
cut. A marinade will
take a long time to pen-
etrate a very dense
piece of meat or a very
large one—plan on at
least overnight, and up
to several days is ok.
The acid will cause the
meat to look gray, but
that is fine. Something
delicate, like fish, is
best marinated briefly,
as the acid gives fish a
cooked texture if mari-
nated more than a few
hours. If the piece is
not dense, like fish, or
if it has been cut up,
you can reduce the
time to as little as an
hour or two.

These chicken thighs are slightly sweet and slightly hot. The grill contributes a nice smoky flavor, but if need be the broiler can be used very successfully. Boneless thighs are very tender and easy to eat; you can remove the skin if you like. They can even be threaded on skewers before cooking. This freezes for up to 3 months. Reheat in foil, thawed, in a preheated 350° F. oven 20 to 30 minutes.

1 cup honey
1/4 cup sesame seeds
1 teaspoon ground ginger
1 teaspoon ground cinnamon
1 teaspoon ground cumin
1 teaspoon paprika
1/2 teaspoon turmeric (optional)

1/2 teaspoon cayenne pepper
3 tablespoons fresh lime juice
2 tablespoons olive oil
Salt
Freshly ground black pepper
12 boneless chicken thighs

In a large bowl, combine the honey, sesame seeds, ginger, cinnamon, cumin, paprika, turmeric, cayenne, lime juice, and olive oil. Season to taste with salt and pepper. Pour over the chicken thighs and marinate, covered, overnight in the refrigerator. When ready to cook, remove the chicken from the marinade and grill about 6 to 8 minutes on each side, being careful not to let the flames flare up. If broiling, place on a greased baking sheet and cook 5 inches from the heat.

Serves 6

PIERRE-HENRI'S
LEMON CHICKEN

What a delight it was when Pierre-Henri and Audrey came home to live with me! Pierre-Henri's parents once lived in Morocco, and he has introduced many of his mother's recipes into my kitchen. This dish is ridiculously simple for something so delicious. It may be made in advance and makes great leftovers. We prefer thighs, but you may prefer a cut-up chicken. The preserved lemon adds so much flavor to this dish, but no additional calories, and the butter may be omitted with only a minor flavor loss. If you have no preserved lemons, see the variation below. The recipe doubles easily and freezes for up to 4 months.

3 pounds chicken thighs (or 1 3-pound chicken cut into serving pieces)
2 large onions, finely chopped
2 teaspoons finely chopped fresh ginger
¼ teaspoon crumbled saffron
¼ cup butter or oil (optional)

2 garlic cloves, peeled and finely chopped
1 preserved lemon (page 158), peel only, cut into ¼-inch julienne, then into ¾-inch pieces
10 to 12 large green olives
Salt

Place the chicken, onions, ginger, saffron, butter if using, and garlic in a large Dutch oven. Add water to cover. Bring to the boil over medium heat, then cover, reduce the heat, and simmer until the chicken nearly falls off the bone, about 1 to 1¼ hours. Turn the chicken occasionally so it will absorb the sauce evenly. Add water as needed to keep the chicken covered.

About 10 minutes before the chicken is done, add the lemon peel and olives and continue cooking, uncovered. When the chicken is *very* tender, remove it to a serving platter and set aside. Simmer the sauce over medium heat until it has reduced and thickened to a syrupy consistency, about 20 minutes. Season to taste with salt. Serve with couscous.

Serves 4 to 6

VARIATION: *Instead of lemon peel and olives, add 1 teaspoon chopped fresh cilantro, 1 teaspoon chopped fresh parsley, 1½ teaspoons ground cumin, 1 teaspoon paprika, ½ cup lemon juice, and salt to taste.*

DEVILED CHICKEN

It takes just a few minutes to combine these ingredients and dredge the chicken thighs. This can be done early in the day and left refrigerated until needed. Then into the oven it all goes, cooking for 2 hours without drying out. It's ideal for the kind of day where you have a lot of activities and not much time to accomplish them. This chicken, adapted from a recipe of Laurie Colwin's, is delicious, with every bite tender and full of flavor down to the bone. I use chicken thighs, as they have more flavor and don't dry out during the long cooking process. Store-bought breadcrumbs can be used in a pinch, but homemade are much better. This reheats well for 6 to 8 minutes in a 350°F. oven, but it does not freeze.

1 cup Dijon mustard
3 garlic cloves, peeled and chopped
2 tablespoons chopped fresh rosemary
1 teaspoon pepper

½ teaspoon cinnamon
8 chicken thighs
3 cups dry breadcrumbs

Preheat the oven to 325°F.

In a large bowl, combine the mustard, garlic, rosemary, pepper, and cinnamon. Coat each chicken thigh with the mixture, then roll in breadcrumbs, covering completely. **Can be prepared to this point up to 3 hours in advance and kept refrigerated.**

Bake for 2 hours (yes, 2 hours), or until the chicken is tender and the crust is crisp. Serve hot.

Serves 4 to 6

DUCK WITH ORANGE AND MINT

Few dishes go from summer to winter as easily as this one. It cools in the hot weather, satisfies deliciously in the cool.

1 5- to 6-pound duck
2 oranges
4 sprigs of mint

Salt
Freshly ground black pepper

Preheat the oven to 450°F.

Wash the duck and gently pat dry with paper towels. Prick the duck all over with a fork. Peel the oranges and rub the orange segments over the duck. Place the orange segments in the cavity of the duck with the mint sprigs. Season the entire duck with salt and pepper. Truss the duck. *The trussed duck can be refrigerated for several hours. Bring to room temperature before cooking.* Place the duck on a rack in a roasting pan and place in the oven. Roast for 15 minutes, lower the temperature to 350°F, and cook for 1½ hours. When cool, split or cut down either side of the backbone from neck to tail and divide the duck in 2 pieces. Pull out the breast and rib bones. *At this point the duck can be refrigerated for 2 or 3 days.* To reheat and recrisp the skin, run under the broiler. Serve hot or at room temperature with Pineapple and Orange Salsa (page 154).

Serves 4

ORIENTAL TURKEY LOAF

This meat loaf is very different, taking its flavor from the influences of the Far East. Leftovers (if any) make a wonderful sandwich. This meat loaf is not as dense as a more traditional recipe; therefore, slicing it may be a bit more difficult, particularly when cold. It freezes for up to 4 months.

1 pound ground turkey	*2 tablespoons soy sauce*
1 pound ground veal	*1 teaspoon Oriental sesame oil*
5 green onions, chopped	*2 eggs*
1 tablespoon chopped fresh ginger	*1 7½-ounce jar hoisin sauce*
1 8-ounce can water chestnuts, drained	*½ to ¾ cup breadcrumbs*
2 teaspoons Chinese or Dijon mustard	*½ teaspoon hot red pepper flakes*

Preheat the oven to 375° F. Grease a 9 × 5 × 3-inch loaf pan.

In a large bowl, combine the turkey, veal, green onions, ginger, water chestnuts, Chinese mustard, soy sauce, sesame oil, eggs, ½ cup of the hoisin sauce, the breadcrumbs, and red pepper flakes, mixing with a wooden spoon or your hands. Shape the mixture into a loaf and place it in the prepared pan. Bake for 30 minutes. Remove from the oven and spread the remaining hoisin sauce over the top. Cover loosely with foil and return to the oven for 30 to 40 minutes longer. Remove from the oven and let cool in the pan for 10 minutes before slicing. Serve warm.

Serves 6 to 8

TURKEY BREAST PISTOU

Pesto sauce is now so readily available in the grocery store that I save my homemade for special occasions. Storebought is fine for this recipe, which just bursts with the flavors of basil, lemons, and tomatoes. The blend makes an unbeatable, harmonious gravy for the turkey. I make the marinade one day, bake the turkey the next, and either put the turkey in the oven before church and serve it shortly after noon or roast it a day ahead of time and reheat it for 30 to 45 minutes at 350° F.

½ cup fresh lemon juice
Grated peel (no white attached) of 3
   lemons
½ cup Pesto Sauce (page 155)
2 teaspoons prepared horseradish
¼ cup sun-dried tomatoes packed in oil,
   drained and chopped

1 6-pound turkey breast
½ teaspoon salt
½ teaspoon freshly ground black
   pepper
2 cups fresh or canned chicken stock or
   broth

In a large bowl, mix together the lemon juice, peel, pesto, horseradish, and sun-dried tomatoes. Rub this mixture on the turkey breast and let it marinate in the refrigerator 24 hours.

Preheat the oven to 350° F.

Place the turkey breast in a pan, sprinkle with salt and pepper, and add enough stock to come 1 inch up the side of the pan. Bake for 2 to 2½ hours, or until a meat thermometer registers 180° F. Transfer the breast to a cutting board and let sit 10 minutes before slicing thinly. **The turkey can be refrigerated for 3 to 4 days.** Skim the excess fat off the pan juices and bring to the boil on top of the stove. Continue to boil until reduced by half, about 10 minutes. Arrange the turkey slices on a platter and pass the gravy separately.

Serves 8

TURKEY CROQUETTES

Here is an excellent way to use up leftovers from the holidays. If there is not enough turkey left on the carcass, substitute any remaining dressing for the turkey cup for cup. And top the croquettes with leftover gravy.

2 celery stalks, chopped	Salt
1 red bell pepper, roasted, peeled, seeded, and chopped	Freshly ground black pepper
	6 cups chopped cooked turkey
6 green onions, chopped	¾ cup cranberry sauce, whole or jellied
2 teaspoons fresh lemon juice	2 eggs, beaten
3 tablespoons chopped fresh parsley	1 cup cracker crumbs
2 teaspoons dried sage	Turkey gravy
1 teaspoon poultry seasoning	

Preheat the oven to 350° F. Grease a baking sheet.

In a large bowl, combine the celery, red pepper, green onions, lemon juice, parsley, sage, poultry seasoning, salt, pepper, turkey, cranberry sauce, and eggs. Mix well. Cover the bowl and chill for at least 45 minutes. *Can be refrigerated up to 24 hours at this point.*

Shape the croquette mixture into 10 ovals, roll in cracker crumbs, and place on a greased baking sheet. *The shaped croquettes can be refrigerated for up to 4 hours.* Bake 20 minutes, or until golden. Serve at once with hot gravy.

Serves 8

TURKEY TONNATO

This dish is a variation of the classic veal dish but made with inexpensive turkey. The silky smooth sauce is even better the next day and the turkey may be cooked and refrigerated or frozen ahead as well. I assemble it up to a day in advance, keeping it refrigerated as much as possible. Turkey Tonnato is perfect for picnics as well as elegant summer dinners. It freezes well for up to 4 months without the sauce.

TONNATO SAUCE
1 cup mayonnaise
2 7-ounce cans tuna in water, drained
6 anchovy fillets
½ to ¾ cup olive oil
¼ cup fresh lemon juice
2 tablespoons drained capers

Freshly ground black pepper
1 5- to 6-pound turkey breast, cooked

GARNISH
2 lemons, sliced
About 12 cornichons, halved

In a food processor or blender, combine the mayonnaise, tuna, anchovies, olive oil, lemon juice, and capers. Season to taste with pepper. Process until smooth.

Slice the turkey breast off the bone into thin slices and arrange on a platter, overlapping one another. Pour the sauce over the turkey. Garnish the sides of the platter with the lemon slices, alternating with the halved cornichons. Serve chilled or at room temperature.

Serves 6 to 8

**TO POACH A
TURKEY
BREAST**
Once I bought what was called boneless breast of turkey and it turned out to be a pressed loaf of some sort, very disappointing to slice—and to eat! Since then, I have generally preferred to poach my own turkey breast, which is both easy and more economical.

Place the turkey breast in a 5-quart stockpot with a carrot, an onion, 2 parsley sprigs, a bay leaf, and 10 peppercorns. Add enough water to cover, bring to the boil, reduce the heat, and simmer, covered, about 2 hours. Skim off any scum that may rise to the surface. Allow the breast to cool in the stock. The stock may then be refrigerated for several days or frozen and used like any turkey or chicken broth. I use it for regular turkey gravy at holiday time. Use the turkey for sandwiches, salads, casseroles, or the like.

BAKED HERBED FISH FILLETS

It's ever so nice to bread these fillets ahead of time, leaving them flat on a baking sheet in the fridge, then run them under the preheated broiler for just 3 minutes before turning and finishing. The fish is firm but moist, and the nuts are brown enough to perfume the fish. Heat your vegetables in the microwave while the fish broils and dinner's on the table!

Remember, broiling, grilling, or baking any type of fish 10 minutes per inch of thickness is a good rule to go by.

6 to 8 fish fillets (catfish, trout, flounder), about 6 ounces each	*2 tablespoons chopped fresh chives*
½ cup pecans, finely ground	*1 teaspoon chopped fresh oregano*
¾ cup breadcrumbs	*Salt*
1 tablespoon grated lime peel (no white attached)	*Freshly ground black pepper*
1 tablespoon grated lemon peel (no white attached)	*4 to 6 tablespoons butter, melted*
	2 tablespoons fresh lemon juice
	Lemon wedges

Preheat the grill or broiler. Lightly butter a broiler pan.

With a paper towel, pat the fillets dry. In a shallow bowl, mix together the pecans, breadcrumbs, lime peel, lemon peel, chives, oregano, and salt and pepper to taste. In a small saucepan, melt the butter with the lemon juice. Brush the fillets on each side with the melted lemon butter, then dip them into the breadcrumb mixture, coating each side evenly. Place the fish fillets on a broiler pan. ***The breaded fillets can be covered tightly with plastic wrap and refrigerated for 2 to 3 hours.***

Just before serving, preheat the broiler. Broil the fillets 2 to 3 minutes per side, or until the fish is opaque. Serve at once with fresh lemon wedges.

Serves 6

BAKED OR MICROWAVED FILLETS OF FLOUNDER WITH MOROCCAN SPICES

The Moroccan sauce *chermoula* was the inspiration for this dish's assertive seasonings. In my version of *chermoula*, I eliminated the oil and added some of my own favorite spices to make a flavorful spice rub that is equally good on baked or microwaved fish. It makes its own lovely saffrony sauce and is very low in calories and fat.

SPICE RUB

½ teaspoon ground ginger
2 tablespoons chopped fresh coriander
1 teaspoon ground cumin
1 teaspoon ground anise
1 tablespoon chopped fresh parsley
2 tablespoons fresh lemon juice

¼ teaspoon crumbled saffron
Peel of 1 preserved lemon (page 158),
  chopped

4 6-ounce fillets white fish or flounder

In a small bowl, combine the ginger, coriander, cumin, anise, parsley, lemon juice, saffron, and 2 tablespoons of the preserved lemon peel and mix well. Rub the mixture onto both sides of the fillets and place on a flat dish. Cover with plastic wrap and marinate for at least 2 hours or up to 6 hours in the refrigerator.

Preheat the oven to 350°F. Transfer the fillets to a baking sheet and bake, uncovered, for 5 minutes per inch of thickness. Alternatively, cover with plastic wrap and cook in the microwave on High for 2 to 4 minutes, according to thickness. Serve hot.

Serves 4

SALAD OF POACHED FISH
WITH GRAPES

POACHING FISH
Poaching is gentle, preserves moisture, and can add flavor. You can poach any type of fish, but because the method is easily controlled, it is well suited to delicate pieces, such as fillets of sole. Since you can see the tiny bubbles, you can tell the approximate temperature. The poaching liquid cannot get above 212° F. by more than a few degrees, no matter how long you leave it on the heat. And, of course, additions such as anise or garlic will affect the flavor of the dish.

> 2 quarts water
> 4 stems of parsley
> 2 lemon wedges
> 10 peppercorns
> 1 small onion, halved
> 1 teaspoon salt
> 1 teaspoon white
>   wine vinegar

In a Dutch oven, combine the water, parsley, lemon, peppercorns, onion, salt, and vinegar. Heat to the boiling point, then reduce the heat to a simmer. Gently add the fish fillets and poach for about 8 minutes with the water barely at a simmer. Remove the fillets with a slotted spoon and drain on paper towels.

I invented this recipe one hot day when I yearned for a classic Véronique sauce but wanted something less rich. It's light and fresh, perfect for a luncheon. The grapes add a subtle sweetness and the almonds a very pleasing crunch. The recipe can be made with almost any type of cooked fish, and the entire recipe may be made a couple of days in advance if the fish is very fresh, but add the almonds just before serving, as they lose their crunch. This does not freeze.

6 firm fish fillets, such as grouper or red
  snapper
¾ cup mayonnaise
1 teaspoon fresh lemon juice
¾ cup heavy cream
Grated peel (no white attached) of
  1 orange
2 tablespoons fresh orange juice
1½ cups halved or quartered red or green
  seedless grapes
Salt
Freshly ground black pepper
Pinch of freshly grated nutmeg
½ cup sliced toasted almonds

Arrange the fish fillets in a Dutch oven with water to cover. Poach gently just until done (see sidebar), then drain and refrigerate until chilled.

In a medium bowl, mix together the mayonnaise, lemon juice, cream, orange peel, juice, and 1¼ cups of the grapes. Season to taste with the salt, pepper, and nutmeg. Cover tightly and store in the fridge until just before serving. *The fish and the dressing can be made a day or 2 in advance.*

To serve, arrange the cooked fish in a shallow serving bowl. Stir the almonds into the sauce, gently spoon over the cooled fish fillets, and serve garnished with additional grapes, if desired.

Serves 6

BAKED MOROCCAN SWORDFISH STEAKS WITH LEMONS AND ONION CONFIT

Late one night I was reading a Joyce Goldstein recipe in bed. She described a fish with onion confit and lemons that made my mouth water as I thought about it at 2 A.M., but it called for lemons preserved in sugar, which must be prepared twenty-four hours in advance. However, waiting in my kitchen were Pierre-Henri's beautiful fat lemons preserved in brine, showing off in a glass jar. In the morning, I used them and had this wonderful dish for lunch. It lived up to every expectation and then some. What I like, though, is that the whole dish may be totally assembled ahead of time and baked at the end of a busy day.

TAMING LONG INGREDIENT LISTS
Recently a woman told me she'd never cook a particular recipe of mine because she was daunted by the long ingredient list. A large number of ingredients doesn't necessarily mean more preparation time, particularly if you have a food processor or blender—it just means more flavor and diversity. Sometimes, I think the more ingredients, the easier. I don't chop everything separately but just throw it *all* in the food processor at once!

MARINADE
½ teaspoon saffron
½ cup fresh lemon juice
½ cup chopped fresh parsley
½ cup chopped fresh cilantro
6 garlic cloves, peeled and finely chopped
1 tablespoon paprika
2 teaspoons ground cumin
½ teaspoon cayenne pepper
4 swordfish steaks (¾ to 1 inch thick) or
  grouper fillets

ONION CONFIT
6 tablespoons (¾ stick) butter
6 large onions, thinly sliced

4 teaspoons ground ginger
½ teaspoon turmeric
1 teaspoon ground cumin
1 tablespoon paprika
1 teaspoon ground coriander
Salt
Freshly ground black pepper
1 large preserved lemon (page 158), peel
  removed and chopped

GARNISH
24 kalamata or other black Greek-type
  olives
4 tablespoons olive oil
2 garlic cloves, peeled and crushed

To prepare the marinade, crumble the saffron in a small bowl. Add the lemon juice and stir. Add the parsley, cilantro, garlic, paprika, cumin, and cayenne. Rub on both sides of the fish steaks and marinate for about 1 hour or overnight in a large oiled plastic bag in the refrigerator.

To prepare the confit, melt the butter in a very large skillet over medium heat. Add the onions and cook over low heat until very soft, about 20 minutes, covering if necessary. Stir in the ginger, turmeric, cumin, paprika, and coriander, and cook a few more minutes. Season to taste with salt and pepper. Stir in 2 tablespoons of the preserved lemon peel and set aside to cool. *The confit can be made several days ahead or frozen up to 2 weeks.*

Place the steaks in an oiled baking dish. Spoon the onion mixture over the steaks. *This can be refrigerated for an hour or 2.*

When ready to cook, preheat the oven to 400°F. Measure the thickness of the fish, including the onion topping, and bake about 15 minutes per inch of thickness, or until the fish is cooked.

While the fish is baking, prepare the olive garnish. Remove the pits from the olives and cut them in wedges. Place in a bowl and add the olive oil, garlic, and the remaining 2 tablespoons preserved lemon peel; let stand at room temperature.

When the fish is cooked, transfer to a serving plate and garnish with the olives.

Serves 4 to 6

SMOKED TROUT

Smoked fish is delicious in salads, pâtés, and on its own. This recipe uses trout, but you could substitute nearly any other fish, including salmon or bluefish.

Smoking chips   *1½ pounds whole trout*

Place the chips in the bottom of your smoker. Place the trout on the rack of the smoker and cover tightly. Smoke for about 25 minutes. Check for doneness. The fish should register 150°F. to 170°F. on a meat thermometer. Cool, then wrap well and refrigerate for 3 or 4 days.

Serves 2 to 4

SALMON WITH TOMATO-CREAM SAUCE

 This dish has finesse and elegance with a touch of the unusual. On occasion I have omitted the cream and butter and found it works surprisingly well.

2 tablespoons butter or olive oil
1 medium onion, sliced
1 1-pound can whole tomatoes, crushed,
   and their juice
1 1¾- to 2-pound salmon fillet
Juice of 1 lime

½ to 1 teaspoon ground cumin, or to
   taste
Salt
Freshly ground black pepper
1 cup heavy cream

Heat the butter in a skillet, add the onion, and cook over medium-low heat until soft, 5 to 7 minutes. Place the sautéed onion in a large baking dish and cover with the slightly broken-up or crushed tomatoes and their juice. Place the fish on top of the tomatoes and measure the thickness of the fillet and tomatoes. *The salmon can be prepared to this point, covered with plastic wrap and refrigerated up to 24 hours. Return to room temperature before baking.*

When ready to cook, preheat the oven to 400°F. Pour the lime juice over the fish, then sprinkle with the cumin, salt, and pepper to taste. Cover the dish with aluminum foil and place in the middle of the oven. Bake 20 to 30 minutes (approximately 10 minutes per inch of thickness), or until just firm. Remove the fish and set aside.

Strain the pan juices into a heavy saucepan, pressing hard to extract as much juice as possible. Add the heavy cream, bring to the boil, and cook until reduced by about half (see sidebar).

Cut the fish into serving pieces and serve warm with the sauce.

Serves 6 to 8

REDUCING A LIQUID
The purpose of reducing a liquid is to concentrate its flavor and to thicken it. How long the process will take depends on the intensity of the heat, the size (width) of your pan, and, of course, the amount of liquid. It is best to use a heavy-bottomed pan for all reductions to ensure even heat distribution.

If the heat is low, it will take longer to reduce the liquid. Stock can be reduced on high heat. A cream sauce can be boiled down, but you run the risk of scorching it if the heat is too high or the pot too thin. You can use a high heat if you have the time to stir.

If the pan is shallow and wide, the liquid will boil off faster than from a narrow one. So, if you are in a hurry—and don't mind messing up another pot—transfer the liquid into a wide, shallow pan. If you can use the time and don't want to worry about the liquid boiling off too fast, use a deeper pan.

SHRIMP WITH SPICY PEANUT SAUCE OR DIP

Not only does this zippy sauce have the personality to hold its own at a party as a dip for boiled shrimp, it can be pulled out of the refrigerator and used as a sauce for grilled poultry, meat, kebabs, or even rice. I particularly like it with shrimp cooked in this lemon and soy sauce–flavored mixture.

PEANUT SAUCE
2 tablespoons finely chopped fresh ginger
2 garlic cloves, peeled and chopped
⅓ cup red wine vinegar
⅓ cup creamy peanut butter
2 teaspoons hot red pepper flakes
½ cup soy sauce

3 to 4 cups water
1 lemon, sliced
½ cup soy sauce
1½ pounds large shrimp

In a blender or food processor, combine the ginger, garlic, vinegar, peanut butter, red pepper flakes, and soy sauce. Process until well blended and chill. ***The sauce can be made and refrigerated up to 2 days in advance.***

In a large saucepan, bring the water to the boil with the lemon slices and soy sauce. Drop in the shrimp, reduce the heat to a simmer, and cook 2 to 3 minutes, or until they turn pink. Drain, peel, and devein the shrimp. Chill them until ready to serve. ***The cooked shrimp can be refrigerated up to 2 to 3 days.***

To serve, arrange the shrimp on a platter with a bowl of the sauce and toothpicks.

Serves 6 to 8

GRAVLAX

Gravlax, a Swedish specialty, is a simple but elegant preparation for fish. Salmon and trout are my favorites. It may take you all of five minutes to prepare this. In Finland, at the outdoor fish stands next to Helsinki's port, it is done by the fishermen so quickly for their customers it seems magical. You may serve gravlax as a first course for a dinner party or on crackers or toast points with sour cream and capers for cocktails. Either way, it's a hit with guests.

1 tablespoon salt	*1 12-ounce salmon or trout fillet*
2 tablespoons sugar	*(see Note)*
12 crushed black peppercorns	*1 bunch fresh dill*

Sprinkle the salt, sugar, and black peppercorns in a plastic wrap–lined large 9 × 13-inch roasting pan. Let the plastic wrap overlap enough to ultimately enclose the salmon completely. Lay the salmon, skin-side up, on top of the mixture and cover the fillet with large sprigs of dill. Fold in the sides of plastic wrap to cover and set a board on top. Cover loosely and refrigerate for 2 days, turning the salmon about every 12 hours and basting with the juices. Discard the dill and drain the fish. Rewrap until ready to serve. The marinated fish keeps for several days in the refrigerator. Slice thinly to serve.

Serves 4

N O T E : *A whole salmon side can be prepared in this way simply by increasing the amount of seasonings.*

Jim Landon's Baked Asparagus ■ *Chunky Applesauce with Caramelized Onions* ■ *Stuffed Bell Peppers* ■ *Lu Len's Slow-Roasted Peppers* ■ *Steamed Brussels Sprouts and Carrots with Honey Mustard Sauce* ■ *Sesame Cabbage and Green Beans* ■ *Grilled Carrots and Broccoli* ■ *Cauliflower with Curry Sauce* ■ *Sautéed Fennel and Zucchini* ■ *Mapled Acorn Squash* ■ *Stuffed Summer Squash* ■ *Greek-Style Green Beans* ■ *Finnish Peas in the Pod* ■ *Make-Ahead Coriander Green Beans* ■ *Caramelized Green Onions and Carrots* ■ *Garlic-Rosemary Red Potatoes*

VEGETABLES & MEATLESS MAIN COURSES

■ *Baked and Mashed Sweet Potatoes* ■ *Orange Oven-Roasted Potatoes* ■ *Roasted Salted Fan Potatoes* ■ *Oven-Browned Potatoes and Onions* ■ *Stuffed Tomatoes with Spinach and Yogurt Cheese* ■ *Tomato Bake* ■ *Pureed Winter Vegetable Treat* ■ *Grilled Vegetables with Parmesan and Balsamic Vinegar* ■ *Tomato-Fennel Casserole* ■ *Lemon Corn Bread Dressing* ■ *Macaroni and Cheese with Sun-Dried Tomatoes* ■ *New Southwestern Corn Pudding* ■ *Baked Pasta and Zucchini* ■ *Baked Onion Soup Casserole* ■ *Sesame Noodles with Broccoli* ■ *Pasta with Sweet Onion Sauce*

WHEN I'M TRAVELING, I start to fantasize about vegetables. Although abroad I often find vegetarian plates on menus, when in the small U.S. cities that are on my regular beaten path, I find myself starved for vegetables and crave them.

So when I am home, vegetables are the first thing I cook. Why it is hard to find a good baked or boiled potato in a restaurant is beyond me. But at home, they are my mainstays. Sometimes that's all I'll eat for a solitary meal, slathered with Maître d'Hôtel Butter (page 156), perhaps. And whether on their own or as an accompaniment to turkey or pork roast, baked and mashed sweet potatoes stay in the mind a long time.

Much as I love vegetables though, I'm not a believer in rushing around and doing the vegetable portion of the meal at the last minute, throwing off the timing of the meal. I try to get some of the preparation done in advance, whether it is slicing zucchini or roasting a pepper while I'm cooking something else. I prepare many of my vegetables in large quantities and use them in several meals. String beans lend themselves to this, as do broccoli and cauliflower.

I may reheat a portion in the microwave at one meal or toss with butter and seasonings in a sauté pan at another. And I have come to depend on substantial and nourishing casseroles of vegetables (often with a cheesy topping or flavoring) to serve as the focal point of the meal when there are vegetarian guests in the crowd.

JIM LANDON'S BAKED ASPARAGUS

Miraculously, this is a green vegetable dish that requires no last-minute prep. It's ideal for times when the stove top is full or the oven is already on. Jim Landon was a cooking student of mine years ago.

2 pounds thin asparagus

¼ to ½ cup (½ to 1 stick) butter

Salt

Freshly ground black pepper

Preheat the oven to 350°F.

Spread a long piece of aluminum foil on a baking sheet and spread the asparagus on the foil, 2 or 3 spears high. Dot with butter and season to taste with salt and pepper. Cover tightly with more foil. Bake 30 minutes. Serve hot or at room temperature.

Serves 6 to 8

CHUNKY APPLESAUCE WITH CARAMELIZED ONIONS

Serve this tasty side dish with potato latkes and turkey croquettes after Thanksgiving—a great opportunity for leftovers to dazzle!

¼ cup (½ stick) butter

1 medium onion, coarsely chopped

8 large apples

Salt

Freshly ground black pepper

Melt the butter in a large skillet over medium heat. Add the onion and sauté until golden, about 5 minutes.

While the onion is sautéing, peel, core, and thinly slice the apples. Add the apples to the skillet and toss together with the onion. Cover the skillet and cook over low heat, stirring occasionally, until the apples are tender, about 15 minutes. Season to taste with salt and pepper. Serve warm.

Serves 6 to 8

STUFFED BELL PEPPERS

These peppers are halved lengthwise and then stuffed. This makes an attractive presentation that is just right for a side dish. These peppers are particularly good accompanying roast lamb or pork. Try stuffing the mixture into a hollowed-out tomato or blanched onion for an interesting variation. The peppers may be made ahead a couple of days, but I also have made the filling one day and blanched the peppers another, combining and reheating when they were to be served. They reheat in the microwave for 3 to 4 minutes.

2 tablespoons olive oil	4 scallions or green onions, green parts
2 tablespoons butter	only, chopped, or ¼ cup chopped
2 teaspoons curry powder	chives
1 large onion, chopped	¼ cup chopped fresh parsley
3 garlic cloves, peeled and chopped	2 tablespoons chopped fresh oregano or
1 cup long-grain rice	thyme or 1 tablespoon dried
4 cups fresh or canned chicken stock or	Salt
broth, simmering	Freshly ground black pepper
½ cup raisins	3 red or green peppers, halved lengthwise,
	seeds and membranes removed

Preheat the oven to 350°F.

In a large skillet, heat the oil and butter until bubbling. Add the curry powder, onion, garlic, and rice and cook for 2 minutes. Add 3 cups of the hot chicken stock and bring to the boil. Cover, reduce the heat to a simmer, and cook for 20 minutes. Add the raisins, scallions, 2 tablespoons of the parsley, the oregano, and salt and pepper to taste. ***The peppers can be made several hours ahead to this point or frozen until needed.***

Meanwhile, blanch the pepper halves in 5 quarts of boiling salted water for 2 minutes. Remove and drain. Alternatively, they may be microwaved until nearly tender. ***The blanched peppers can be refrigerated up to 2 days.***

Divide the rice mixture among the pepper halves and place them in a shallow roasting pan. Pour in enough chicken stock to come halfway up the peppers, cover the pan with foil, and bake 25 minutes. Remove the foil and bake 10 minutes more. Sprinkle with the remaining 2 tablespoons parsley before serving.

Serves 6

LU LEN'S SLOW-ROASTED PEPPERS

This medley is best made in the fall, when the bell peppers and chile peppers turn flaming red. It can be used as a spread on a thick slice of bread, as a colorful bed for grilled fowl or fish, or as a sauce with pasta or a few strips of meat. I've substituted green chile peppers as well as hot red pepper flakes, and I like to double or triple the recipe, as it keeps in the refrigerator very well for 2 or 3 weeks. Best of all, it requires virtually no work—it's all dumped in a pan and left to cook, with just one stir after an hour. But it is so special that I cooked it for my friend Lu Len's wedding. You may add balsamic vinegar if you wish. If you don't have time to roast and peel the peppers, I've done this many times with unpeeled and it works fine. Divided in half, this serves 6.

16 red peppers, preferably roasted,
  peeled, seeded, and cut into wide strips
6 jalapeño peppers, seeded and chopped
4 large onions, sliced

30 garlic cloves, peeled and chopped
¼ cup olive oil
Salt
Freshly ground black pepper

Preheat the oven to 400°F.

In two 9 × 13-inch baking dishes, combine the red peppers, jalapeño peppers, onions, garlic, and olive oil. Season to taste with salt and pepper. Cover with foil and bake 1 hour. Remove the foil, stir the peppers, and bake, uncovered, 1 hour longer, until the peppers begin to char and brown. Remove from the oven and serve warm or at room temperature.

Serves 12

STEAMED BRUSSELS SPROUTS AND CARROTS WITH HONEY MUSTARD SAUCE

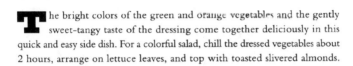

The bright colors of the green and orange vegetables and the gently sweet-tangy taste of the dressing come together deliciously in this quick and easy side dish. For a colorful salad, chill the dressed vegetables about 2 hours, arrange on lettuce leaves, and top with toasted slivered almonds.

2 pounds baby carrots, peeled	*2 tablespoons chopped fresh cilantro*
2 pounds Brussels sprouts, washed, ends	*2 tablespoons chopped celery leaves*
scored with an **X**	*(optional)*
½ cup (1 stick) butter, melted	*1 tablespoon mustard seeds*
¼ cup Dijon mustard	*Salt*
¼ cup honey	*Freshly ground black pepper*

Place the carrots in a vegetable steamer over boiling water. Cover and cook over medium heat 10 to 15 minutes, or until the carrots are just becoming tender. Add the Brussels sprouts, cover, and cook for about 7 minutes longer, or until the vegetables are crisp-tender. Remove the vegetables and place in a large bowl. *The vegetables can be refrigerated for a day or 2.*

Combine the butter, mustard, honey, cilantro, celery leaves if using, and mustard seeds. Season to taste with salt and pepper. Toss the dressing with the warm vegetables and let sit 15 minutes for the flavors to develop. Serve at room temperature, cold, or reheat and serve hot.

Serves 8 to 10

SESAME CABBAGE AND GREEN BEANS

It's amazing how different cabbage can taste when featured in different cuisines. This Oriental rendition is particularly nice as part of an all-vegetable meal or with ham and pork. For make-ahead meals it is served at room temperature, but it's also nice hot.

1 pound green beans, tipped and tailed
2 tablespoons peanut oil
¼ head red cabbage, shredded
1 teaspoon sugar (optional)

2 tablespoons soy sauce
2 teaspoons dark Oriental sesame oil
Freshly ground black pepper
1 tablespoon sesame seeds

Bring a large saucepan of water to the boil. Add the beans and blanch for 3 to 5 minutes, drain, refresh under cold running water, and drain again. *The beans can be blanched and refrigerated up to 3 days in advance.*

Heat the oil in a large skillet until quite hot. Add the cabbage and blanched beans and sauté just until the cabbage wilts but is still crisp, about 5 minutes. In a small bowl, combine the sugar if using, soy sauce, sesame oil, and pepper to taste. Add to the cabbage-bean mixture and toss to coat. Sprinkle with the sesame seeds, and serve hot or at room temperature.

Serves 4 to 6

GRILLED CARROTS
AND BROCCOLI

This grilled combo was inspired by a local restaurant menu and is a low-calorie favorite of all of ours as well as an interesting conversation piece. The majority of the work involved is done with the first step, which may be done 1 to 2 days in advance. Grilling adds panache to what would otherwise be mundane. I cook this on my stovetop grill as well as outdoors.

4 medium-large carrots, peeled	2 to 3 tablespoons olive oil
1 head broccoli, stems peeled and	Salt
trimmed, left whole	Freshly ground black pepper

Cook the carrots and broccoli individually until soft but not mushy, about 5 minutes in the microwave. Or bring a large pan of water to the boil, add the carrots and cook 5 minutes, then add the broccoli and cook 5 minutes longer. Drain the vegetables, refresh under cold water, and drain again. *This can be done up to several days in advance*.

When ready to serve, brush the vegetables lightly with oil and cook them on a hot grill, turning frequently, until lightly charred on the outside and tender inside, 3 to 7 minutes. Season to taste with salt and pepper and serve hot or at room temperature.

Serves 4

CAULIFLOWER WITH CURRY SAUCE

COOKING VEGETABLES AHEAD
Almost any vegetable can be cooked ahead and reheated at serving time. The only real danger is in overcooking them. Tender vegetables—such as asparagus, broccoli, small green beans, or snow peas—should be put into a large pot of boiling water for just 3 to 4 minutes, then drained and refreshed in cold water. This bath will stop the cooking and will set their color. Cauliflower can be "blanched" the same way. Root vegetables—potatoes, carrots, turnips, and the like—should be put into cold water and brought to the boil. They too should be put into cold water to stop the cooking when they are still underdone, 15 to 20 minutes perhaps, depending on how they are cut. The vegetables can be reheated by tossing with hot butter, in the microwave, by dropping into boiling water, or by steaming. The choice of method depends on the needs of the final dish. They may be kept at room temperature for up to several hours or refrigerated for up to 5 days.

Cauliflower touched with the golden color of curry powder makes a beautiful presentation. The head can be separated into florets and the sauce poured over them if desired, but I prefer to leave the cauliflower whole. It reheats well in the microwave.

1 head cauliflower	Salt
2 tablespoons butter	Freshly ground black pepper
2 tablespoons all-purpose flour	¾ cup breadcrumbs tossed with
2 teaspoons curry powder	1 tablespoon melted butter
1 cup milk, at the boil	

Bring 3 to 4 quarts of water to the boil in a large pot. Add the whole head of cauliflower and blanch for 7 to 8 minutes. Drain. *The blanched cauliflower can be refrigerated up to 3 days.*

Preheat the oven to 375°F.

In a small saucepan, melt the butter over medium-high heat. Stir in the flour and cook about 1 minute, stirring constantly, to make a roux. Add the curry powder and cook 2 minutes more. Slowly add the hot milk and whisk over medium heat until boiling and thick, 3 minutes. Reduce the heat and simmer 2 to 3 minutes. Add salt and pepper to taste. *The sauce can be made in advance and refrigerated up to 3 days. Cover with plastic wrap until ready to reheat.*

Place the cauliflower in a deep soufflé dish. Pour the sauce over the cauliflower. *This can be done an hour or 2 in advance.* Top with the breadcrumbs and bake 15 to 20 minutes, until heated through.

Serves 4 to 6

SAUTÉED FENNEL AND ZUCCHINI

This fast sauté is a quick and easy side dish for just about any meat or fish entrée. It can be made in advance and reheated. For a salad variation, serve chilled, tossed with fresh fennel fronds for garnish.

1 tablespoon olive oil
2 fennel bulbs, thinly sliced
3 to 4 zucchini, sliced
1 tablespoon balsamic vinegar

1 tablespoon chopped fresh oregano
Salt
Freshly ground black pepper
¼ cup toasted pine nuts

In a large skillet, heat the oil over medium-high heat. Add the fennel and zucchini and cook, stirring constantly, until the vegetables are cooked through but still crisp-tender, about 7 to 8 minutes. Stir in the vinegar and oregano and season to taste with salt and pepper. *This can be made ahead and reheated at this point*. Add the pine nuts and cook over medium heat for 2 minutes longer. Serve hot.

Serves 4 to 6

MAPLED ACORN SQUASH

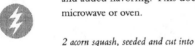

The late fall and early winter seem to call for rich and sweet side dishes. They keep us warm, perhaps, just because they make us think of the holidays. Use 100% pure maple syrup—not the kind that is mostly corn syrup and added flavoring. This does not freeze, but it can be reheated in the microwave or oven.

2 acorn squash, seeded and cut into
  ¾-inch rings
¼ cup (½ stick) butter

¼ cup maple syrup
½ teaspoon freshly grated nutmeg

Preheat the oven to 400°F.

Arrange the squash rings in a glass baking dish, overlapping slightly. In a small skillet, melt the butter. Add the syrup and cook a minute or two, just until bubbly. Pour over the squash and sprinkle with nutmeg. Cover the pan with foil and bake for 30 minutes. Uncover and bake 10 minutes more, or until the squash is brown and tender.

Serves 4 to 6

STUFFED SUMMER SQUASH

I 've always loved a cheesy stuffed squash. I find most people eat 2 or even 3 of these. Leftovers, if any, reheat very well.

10 yellow squash	1 tablespoon chopped fresh thyme or
¼ cup (½ stick) butter	oregano (optional)
1 onion, chopped	Salt
2 garlic cloves, peeled and finely chopped	Freshly ground black pepper
½ cup Yogurt Cheese (page 50)	

Preheat the oven to 350°F.

Cut the squash in half and scoop out the insides, reserving the pulp. Chop 4 of the squash halves and the reserved pulp. Melt the butter in a saucepan over medium heat. Add the onion and garlic and sauté until soft and translucent, about 5 to 7 minutes. Add the chopped squash and cook until soft, about 10 minutes. Stir in the Yogurt Cheese and herbs if using, and season with salt and pepper. Set aside. *This can be made ahead several days to this point.*

Meanwhile, cook the hollowed-out squash halves either in a large pot of boiling water for 10 minutes until nearly soft or in the microwave in a glass dish, loosely covered with wax paper or plastic wrap. Drain. Stuff the drained squash with the sautéed mixture. *The stuffed squash can be made up to 2 days ahead to this point.* When ready to serve, bake 15 minutes, or until heated through.

Serves 4

GREEK-STYLE GREEN BEANS

These beans are just bursting with the flavor of the Mediterranean. They may be served hot as a side dish or at room temperature as a very pleasing starter.

2 pounds green beans, tipped and tailed
3 tablespoons butter
2 garlic cloves, peeled and chopped
1 red bell pepper, seeded and sliced
14 Greek-style olives, drained, pitted,
   and halved

1 tablespoon chopped fresh oregano
2 tablespoons freshly squeezed lemon
   juice
Salt
Freshly ground black pepper

Bring a large quantity of salted water to the boil in a large saucepan. Add the beans and blanch 5 to 7 minutes. Drain, refresh under cold water, and drain again. *This can be done 3 or 4 days in advance.*

In a skillet, heat the butter until it sings. Add the garlic and red pepper and cook until the garlic turns golden, being careful not to let it burn; this will only take a minute or two. Add the blanched beans, olives, oregano, lemon juice, and salt and pepper to taste. Toss for about 2 minutes, until the beans are heated through.

Serves 6 to 8

FINNISH PEAS IN THE POD

Imagine dipping cooked pea pods in butter, then sliding them through your teeth. Discard the pod and swallow the peas. This dish fascinated me when I first heard of it in Helsinki, Finland, where it is a traditional recipe. You may serve it as an hors d'oeuvre or a vegetable. Use the tiniest possible peas. Sugar snap peas are very nice as well.

2 pounds peas in the pod
Salt

¼ to ½ pound (1 to 2 sticks) butter,
   melted

Bring a large pot of water to the boil. Add the peas and salt to taste. Return to the boil and cook, uncovered, 20 minutes. Drain. Refresh under cold water. *This can be made in advance and reheated.* Serve the peas with the melted butter.

Serves 6 to 8

MAKE–AHEAD CORIANDER GREEN BEANS

PUTTING UP BEANS
I put up snap and half-runner green beans in my freezer every summer. I "tip and tail" them (remove the ends) as my mother taught me, stringing them if necessary, then blanch them in boiling water for 5 to 7 minutes. After rinsing under cold water and draining them, I divide them up in freezer containers. When I need them, I defrost them and reheat them in the skillet.

This is a wonderful accompaniment for a simple meal, and is particularly nice as a partner for the rib eye roast (page 59).

1 to 1½ pounds green beans, trimmed	*½ teaspoon sugar*
1 to 2 tablespoons olive oil	*Salt*
1 tablespoon butter	*Freshly ground black pepper*
1½ teaspoons ground coriander	*1 tablespoon toasted sesame seeds*

Place the beans in a large saucepan of boiling water and cook for 5 to 7 minutes. Drain and refresh them in a colander under cold water. *The beans can be refrigerated for 3 or 4 days.*

When ready to serve, heat the olive oil and butter in a large skillet. Add the coriander, sugar, and the beans. Toss well to combine and heat through. Season with salt and pepper to taste. Sprinkle with the sesame seeds and serve at once.

Serves 4 to 6

CARAMELIZED GREEN ONIONS AND CARROTS

The bottom refrigerator drawer tends to collect odd bits of scallions and carrots left over from our recipe testing. One day there were also two rather pitiful endives to add to the collection. By the time the fridge was cleaned, I had a glorious vegetable dish ready to be reheated for dinner. I topped it with a handful of freshly shelled green peas, which was lovely, but even without the endive and peas this is a very nice dish. It reheats well in the microwave.

6 to 8 medium carrots, peeled, halved,
*   and cut to finger length*
2 to 4 tablespoons olive oil
12 scallions or green onions, trimmed to
*   4 or 5 inches*
1 garlic clove, peeled and chopped

1 to 2 small Belgian endives (optional),
*   separated into leaves*
Salt
Freshly ground black pepper
½ cup green peas, cooked and kept warm
*   (optional)*

Cook the carrots in the microwave or place them in a pan of boiling water, cover, and cook over medium-low heat until barely tender, about 8 to 10 minutes. Drain them well. **The carrots can be refrigerated for 2 or 3 days.**

Heat the olive oil until very hot. Add the scallions and carrots and toss in the olive oil until lightly golden. Add the garlic and endive if using and cook until all are lightly browned. Season to taste with salt and pepper, turn into a serving dish, and top with the peas if desired. Serve hot.

Serves 4

GARLIC-ROSEMARY
RED POTATOES

POTATOES
It never hurts to have
some cooked potatoes
on hand, and adding
several more to the pot
will only add minutes to
the cooking time, as it
may take longer for the
water to reach the boil.
Use some for the Garlic-
Rosemary Red Potatoes
and the rest for a pota-
to salad. Or reheat them
and toss with Maître
d'Hôtel Butter (page
156) or another herb
butter.

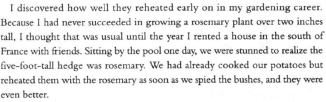

These potatoes are very deceptive, as they taste very fresh but in fact are cooked twice.

I discovered how well they reheated early on in my gardening career. Because I had never succeeded in growing a rosemary plant over two inches tall, I thought that was usual until the year I rented a house in the south of France with friends. Sitting by the pool one day, we were stunned to realize the five-foot-tall hedge was rosemary. We had already cooked our potatoes but reheated them with the rosemary as soon as we spied the bushes, and they were even better.

1½ pounds small red potatoes
2 tablespoons butter
2 tablespoons olive oil
2 garlic cloves, peeled and finely
   chopped

2 teaspoons finely chopped fresh rosemary
1 tablespoon finely chopped fresh parsley
Salt
Freshly ground black pepper

Place the potatoes in a medium saucepan with water to cover. Bring to the boil, reduce the heat to a simmer, and cook until barely tender, about 20 minutes. Drain. If not already small, cut them into 1-inch chunks. *The boiled potatoes can be refrigerated for a day or 2.*

Heat the butter and olive oil in a large frying pan. Add the potatoes and cook, tossing occasionally, for 10 to 15 minutes, or until well browned, adding the garlic for the last 2 to 3 minutes of cooking. Add the rosemary and parsley and toss for a minute longer. Season with salt and pepper to taste.

Serves 4

BAKED AND MASHED
SWEET POTATOES

These are possibly the best sweet potatoes I have ever eaten. The long baking process allows the natural sugars to caramelize and turn an ordinary dish into something quite divine.

4 large sweet potatoes	*Salt*
2 to 4 tablespoons butter	*Freshly ground black pepper*

Preheat the oven to 375° F.

Pierce the sweet potatoes with a fork. Place on a baking sheet and bake for 2 hours (yes, 2 hours). Remove from the oven and set aside to cool.

Peel and mash the sweet potatoes, adding the butter as needed to make a creamy consistency. Season to taste with salt and pepper. Serve hot.

Serves 4 to 6

ORANGE OVEN-ROASTED
POTATOES

These potatoes with their golden crunchy exterior and creamy insides are the perfect accompaniment to fish, roast chicken, or even a hearty cut of beef. They take very little attention from the cook for all the attention they'll get at the table from the eaters. For a unique variation, use sweet potatoes with just a hint of cinnamon.

6 large potatoes, peeled and cut into	*3 tablespoons paprika*
1-inch chunks	*Salt*
2 tablespoons olive oil	*Freshly ground black pepper*
Grated peel (no white attached) of	
1 orange	

Preheat the oven to 400°F.

In a large bowl, toss together the potatoes, olive oil, orange peel, and paprika. Season to taste with salt and pepper. Place in a 13 × 9-inch baking pan and bake about 30 minutes. Stir thoroughly. Continue baking until the potatoes are crispy and golden brown, about 45 minutes longer. Serve at once.

Serves 4 to 6

ROASTED SALTED FAN POTATOES

If you've never made fan potatoes, you'll wish you'd learned about them before. The little slices cause the potato to open up as it cooks and become a fan of slender crisp potatoes. And so little oil is used for such a fantastic dish.

2½ pounds new potatoes, washed　　　　*2 tablespoons kosher salt*
1 to 2 tablespoons olive oil

Preheat the oven to 375°F.

To prepare the potatoes, insert a skewer lengthwise through the potato one-quarter of the way up from the bottom. With a paring knife, make small crosswise cuts ⅛ inch apart through the potato to the skewer. This will create a "fan" effect. Remove the skewer.

In a mixing bowl, toss the potatoes with the oil to coat. Sprinkle with the kosher salt, place the potatoes, cut-side up, in a baking dish, and put in the oven. Bake until tender, 45 to 60 minutes.

Serves 6

OVEN-BROWNED POTATOES
AND ONIONS

 It's amazing how much like crisp potato chips these are with so very little fat. They are usually eaten before they make it off the baking sheets. Don't be tempted to let the potatoes overlap on the baking pans. Each potato needs its own space.

4 baking potatoes, cut into ⅛- to
    ¼-inch slices
2 onions, peeled and cut into ¼-inch
    slices

2 tablespoons olive oil or cooking spray
⅓ teaspoon salt
½ teaspoon pepper
1 teaspoon paprika

Preheat the oven to 425°F. Lightly spray several baking pans with cooking spray.

Spread the potatoes on the pans in a single layer. Scatter the onion slices over the potatoes. Brush with the oil or lightly spray with cooking spray.

Mix together ⅓ teaspoon salt, the pepper, and the paprika. Sprinkle on the potatoes and onions. Bake for 20 minutes, or until the potatoes are golden brown. Add more salt if necessary.

Serves 4

STUFFED TOMATOES WITH SPINACH AND YOGURT CHEESE

This low-cal stuffed tomato is very special and simple. Fixed up to a day ahead of time, it just takes 10 minutes to reheat, having taken not much more than that to assemble. When tomatoes are out of season, microwave or blanch whole onions until soft, hollow them out, and proceed with the recipe.

4 tomatoes
1 tablespoon butter
4 to 6 green onions, chopped
2 garlic cloves, peeled and chopped
1 tablespoon flour
¼ cup freshly grated imported Parmesan cheese
¼ cup breadcrumbs
2 tablespoons chopped fresh herbs (basil, oregano, thyme)

1 10-ounce package frozen spinach, thawed and squeezed to remove moisture
½ cup Yogurt Cheese (page 50)
Salt
Freshly ground black pepper
Nutmeg
Pinch of cayenne pepper
¼ cup freshly grated imported Parmesan cheese (optional)

Preheat the oven to 350° F.

Cut off the flower end of each tomato, leaving the stem end intact. Set aside the cap and hollow out the tomatoes, discarding the pulp. Invert the tomatoes on a plate and drain.

In a nonstick saucepan, melt the butter over low heat. Add the green onions and garlic and sauté until soft, about 3 minutes. Add the flour, Parmesan cheese, breadcrumbs, and herbs. Heat for 1 minute, then add the drained spinach, Yogurt Cheese, and salt, pepper, nutmeg, and cayenne to taste, stirring until well combined. Spoon the spinach mixture into the tomatoes and top with the optional Parmesan if using. *The stuffed tomatoes and their caps can be made to this point up to 3 days in advance.*

Place the tomatoes in an ovenproof serving dish and bake until heated through, about 10 minutes. Top each tomato with the reserved cap and bake 5 minutes more. Serve hot.

Serves 4

TOMATO BAKE

A hollowed-out tomato is as beautiful an individual portion as you can make, and it dresses up a plate of grilled fish or roasted meat very nicely. In summer, when tomatoes are at their peak, bake the tomatoes in the cool of morning, and serve them at room temperature.

6 large tomatoes
3 tablespoons olive oil
1 onion, chopped
2 garlic cloves, peeled and chopped
½ cup breadcrumbs
¼ cup chicken stock
1 teaspoon red wine vinegar

1 tablespoon thyme leaves
1 tablespoon chopped fresh basil
Salt
Freshly ground black pepper
½ cup freshly grated imported Parmesan
  cheese

Preheat the oven to 375°F.

Cut a thin slice off the "flower" end of each tomato. Scoop out the pulp and seeds and chop. Arrange the tomatoes in a buttered casserole so they do not touch. You may have to cut a small slice off the bottom of each to help it stand up.

Heat the oil in a large skillet. Add the onion and garlic and cook over medium-low heat until soft, 8 to 10 minutes. Stir in the chopped tomato pulp, breadcrumbs, chicken stock, vinegar, thyme, basil, and salt and pepper to taste. Fill the tomato shells with the sautéed mixture, mounding slightly. ***The casserole can be covered and refrigerated for up to 3 days at this point***.

Sprinkle each tomato with Parmesan cheese and bake 10 to 12 minutes, until heated through. Serve hot or cool to room temperature.

Serves 6

PUREED WINTER
VEGETABLE TREAT

These root vegetables with their lovely orange color and subtle taste of Dijon and horseradish add a unique dimension to any plate. This is particularly good in the winter when fresh green vegetables are hard to find. It can be reheated especially easily in the microwave or oven.

2 potatoes, peeled and cut into 2-inch chunks

2 sweet potatoes, peeled and cut into 2-inch chunks

2 turnips, peeled and cut into 2-inch chunks

1 rutabaga, peeled and cut into 2-inch chunks

2 onions, peeled and sliced

2 carrots, peeled and sliced

2 tablespoons prepared horseradish

1 tablespoon Dijon mustard

2 tablespoons olive oil

½ to ¾ cup milk

Salt

Freshly ground black pepper

In a large stockpot, combine the potatoes, sweet potatoes, turnips, rutabagas, onions, and carrots with enough salted water to cover by 2 inches. Bring to the boil, reduce the heat, and simmer until the vegetables are very soft, about 1 hour. Drain and return to the pot. With a potato masher or electric mixer, mash the vegetables until fairly smooth but some chunks remain. Stir in the horseradish, mustard, olive oil, and enough milk to make a smooth, creamy consistency. Season to taste with salt and pepper. Serve hot.

Serves 6

GRILLED VEGETABLES WITH PARMESAN AND BALSAMIC VINEGAR

Grilled vegetables are not luxuries in my home—they are staples. They keep up to 5 days in the refrigerator and can be served hot from the grill or broiler, at room temperature (my preference), or chilled. I even eat them at 2:00 A.M., standing in front of the refrigerator when I want "something good"! I also put them on top of pizza and pasta and use them as a bed for meats. Vegetables can also be added to the grill after another meal has been cooked, making two meals in the time of one. If you don't want to heat up the grill, cook the vegetables under the broiler.

4 red bell peppers
2 large onions, peeled and cut into 3-inch wedges, root end intact
2 to 3 tablespoons olive oil
1 large eggplant, halved and degorged (page 143)
3 zucchini, cut lengthwise into ½-inch × ½-inch × 6-inch sticks
2 large firm tomatoes, halved

3 garlic cloves, peeled and chopped
3 tablespoons chopped fresh herbs (basil, rosemary, thyme)
¼ cup balsamic vinegar (optional)
Salt
Freshly ground black pepper
1 cup freshly grated imported Parmesan cheese (optional)

Prepare the grill.

Brush the peppers and onions with a little oil, place the cut side down on the grill, and cook until the peppers are black and charred and the onions are browned or blackened and soft inside.

Remove the peppers from the grill and place them in a plastic bag to steam off the skin. Remove the onions to a large mixing bowl.

Next, brush the cut side of the eggplant with oil, place the cut side down on the grill, and cook until lightly browned and tender but not charred. Remove and add to the bowl with the onions.

Brush the zucchini with oil and add to the grill, cooking until light brown, taking care they don't fall through the grill. Remove and add to the bowl. Brush the tomato halves with oil, place on the grill cut-side down, and cook until tender but not mushy, brushing with oil as needed. Remove from the heat, cut into wedges, and add to the bowl. Remove the red peppers from the plastic bag, peel and seed them, and cut them into ½-inch strips. Add them to the bowl with all the other vegetables. Add the garlic, herbs, balsamic vinegar, salt, and pepper to the bowl with the Parmesan cheese if desired. Toss and serve at room temperature

Serves 6 to 8

TOMATO-FENNEL CASSEROLE

Cooked fennel gives this tomato recipe a lovely underlying flavor of licorice. It's a particularly pretty side dish that reheats well.

3 tablespoons olive oil
3 medium onions, sliced
2 medium-large fennel bulbs, sliced
2 to 3 tablespoons butter
2 cups breadcrumbs

1 28-ounce can whole tomatoes, slightly
broken up
1 teaspoon salt
Freshly ground black pepper

Preheat the oven to 350°F. Grease a 9-inch square baking pan.

Heat the olive oil in a large skillet over medium heat. Add the onions and fennel and cook until soft, 10 to 12 minutes. In another skillet, melt the butter. Add the breadcrumbs and sauté briefly, stirring to combine well.

Place the tomatoes in a mixing bowl and stir in the onions and fennel. Season well with salt and pepper. Pour the vegetables into the prepared baking dish and top with breadcrumbs. ***The dish can be covered and refrigerated for 2 days at this point. Bring to room temperature before baking.***

Bake the casserole 30 to 45 minutes, or until lightly browned. Serve hot.

Serves 6

LEMON CORN BREAD DRESSING

Why make everything the week of a holiday, much less that day? I make this weeks or months ahead of time, label it well, and at the holiday pull it out of the freezer like a magician pulls a bunny out of the hat! Tangy and tart, this dressing is a change of pace from bread stuffing. It's an ideal way to spark up a classic Thanksgiving or special meal. This may be made ahead and reheated, covered with foil. It also freezes well for 2 to 3 months; thaw overnight in the refrigerator before baking.

¼ cup (½ stick) butter

2 large onions, chopped

4 celery stalks, chopped (1 cup)

1½ teaspoons thyme, preferably fresh

½ teaspoon chopped sage, preferably fresh

Grated peel (no white attached) of 2 lemons

4 cups corn bread, broken into large crumbs

3 to 4 cups crumbled biscuit or bread pieces

½ cup dried cherries or cranberries, plumped in warm water for 15 to 20 minutes and drained

1½ tablespoons lemon juice

1 to 1½ cups fresh or canned chicken broth or stock

Salt

Freshly ground black pepper

Preheat the oven to 375°F. Grease a 9-inch square baking pan.

In a large skillet, melt the butter over moderately high heat. Add the onions and celery and cook until soft, about 8 to 10 minutes. Transfer the onions and celery to a large mixing bowl and add the thyme, sage, lemon peel, corn bread, crumbled biscuits, and drained cherries. Combine the lemon juice and chicken stock and stir just enough into the mixture to moisten it well; don't add too much or the dressing will be mushy. Season to taste with salt and pepper. Place the mixture in the prepared pan. Bake 30 to 45 minutes, or until browned.

Serves 4 to 6

MACARONI AND CHEESE WITH SUN-DRIED TOMATOES

TO MAKE BREADCRUMBS
Place the bread in a food processor with a steel knife or a blender and process until medium fine or rub through a strainer for uniform consistency. For dry breadcrumbs, spread out on a baking sheet and toast in a 350°F. oven for 8 to 10 minutes.

This is a wonderful variation on an American classic, updated for the 90s as a main course. (Because it uses less cheese and derives most of its flavor from Italian-inspired ingredients, it is also an excellent side dish to be paired with pork or lamb.) Be careful not to add too much salt, as Parmesan is often quite salty. Use part-skim mozzarella cheese if you want to cut back further on fat and calories. This can be made ahead or frozen for up to 6 months.

3 cups small dried pasta (shells, elbow macaroni, or the like)
1 cup milk
$\frac{1}{2}$ cup grated mozzarella cheese
$\frac{1}{2}$ cup grated imported Parmesan cheese
$\frac{1}{4}$ cup sun-dried tomatoes (not oil-packed), soaked in hot water for 10 minutes, drained, and chopped

$\frac{1}{4}$ cup chopped black olives
$\frac{1}{2}$ teaspoon hot red pepper flakes
1 tablespoon chopped fresh oregano
1 tablespoon chopped fresh parsley
Salt
Freshly ground black pepper
1 cup dry breadcrumbs

Preheat the oven to 375°F.

In a large saucepot, cook the pasta according to package directions. Drain and return to the pot. ***This can be done in advance; toss the pasta with 1 teaspoon oil and refrigerate, covered, for 2 or 3 days.*** Add the milk, mozzarella cheese, Parmesan cheese, sun-dried tomatoes, red pepper flakes, black olives, oregano, and parsley to the cooked pasta. Season to taste with salt and pepper. Stir over medium heat until the sauce thickens and the cheese is melted and smooth, 7 to 10 minutes. Pour the macaroni and sauce into a lightly oiled 13 × 9 × 2-inch pan, top with the breadcrumbs and bake for 20 minutes, or until the top is a nice golden brown.

Serves 6

NEW SOUTHWESTERN
CORN PUDDING

For brunch, Sunday night supper, or even as a side dish, I really enjoy southwestern flavors. You may use whole milk to make the pudding even richer. Other substitutes might be canned corn and chopped canned chile peppers. This reheats well in the microwave.

4 ears corn

1 cup lowfat or skim milk

1½ cups cottage cheese, whirled in a food processor until creamy

½ cup grated Monterey Jack cheese

½ cup grated Cheddar or Colby cheese

4 eggs plus 2 egg whites, lightly beaten

1 medium red onion, chopped (1 cup)

2 to 3 tablespoons chopped fresh green chile peppers

⅓ cup cornmeal mix or self-rising cornmeal

1 tablespoon chopped fresh cilantro

Salt

Freshly ground black pepper

Preheat the oven to 375°F. Butter a 1½-quart soufflé dish.

Cook the corn in the husk for 2 minutes on High in a microwave oven. Cool a minute or two, then remove the husk. Alternatively, place the shucked corn in a large quantity of boiling water until done, about 5 minutes. Using a sharp knife, cut the corn off the cob, then scrape down the cob with the back of the knife to get the "milk" out. Combine the corn, milk, cottage cheese, Monterey Jack cheese, Cheddar cheese, eggs, onion, chile peppers, cornmeal mix, and cilantro. Season to taste with salt and pepper. ***The pudding can be refrigerated for 4 hours at this point.***

Pour the mixture into the prepared soufflé dish. Place a damp kitchen towel in a baking pan. Place the soufflé dish on the towel and add enough hot water to the pan to reach two-thirds of the way up the sides of the dish. Bake for 1 hour, or until the pudding is lightly browned and a cake tester inserted in the center comes out clean. Serve hot.

Serves 6 to 8

BAKED PASTA AND ZUCCHINI

HOW TO "DEGORGE" VEGETABLES
Eggplants, cucumbers, and zucchini taste best when "degorged"—a process used to remove some of the liquid as well as to reduce bitterness. Sprinkle coarse salt on the cut vegetable and set aside in a colander to drain. Rinse off the salt and pat the vegetables dry. If you don't have time for this step, it may be omitted, but do taste the vegetables to be sure they are not bitter. You may need to cook them a bit longer to remove some of the liquid.

This pasta dish is delicious as well as colorful, and very easy to make—all the ingredients are layered in the baking dish.

½ pound colored rotini
1½ pounds zucchini (about 3 medium)
Salt
1 large onion, sliced
½ pound potatoes, peeled and thinly sliced
8 tablespoons (1 stick) butter
4 ounces prosciutto or smoked ham, cut into julienne strips

1½ cups freshly grated imported Parmesan cheese
⅓ cup minced fresh parsley
2 tablespoons chopped fresh basil
1 teaspoon salt
Freshly ground black pepper
1 pound tomatoes (3 medium), peeled and chopped, or 2 cups drained canned plum tomatoes

Preheat the oven to 350°F.

Cook the pasta according to package directions. Drain the pasta and set aside. While the pasta is cooking, trim the zucchini but do not peel. Slice the zucchini thinly, place in a colander, and sprinkle with salt. Let stand at room temperature for 30 minutes to drain off excess moisture.

Put the zucchini between 2 layers of paper towel and squeeze dry with your hands. Place the zucchini in a well-greased 9 × 13-inch clear baking dish. Top with the onion slices, then with the potatoes. Dot with 2 tablespoons of the butter and sprinkle the prosciutto on top. Dot with 2 more tablespoons of butter. Sprinkle ¾ cup Parmesan cheese on top.

In a separate bowl, mix the pasta, parsley, and basil with the salt and pepper to taste. Distribute the pasta over the vegetables in the baking dish. Dot with 2 more tablespoons of butter. Top the pasta with the tomatoes, dot with the remaining butter, and sprinkle the remaining Parmesan on top. *The casserole can be refrigerated for 4 hours at this point.* Cover the baking dish with aluminum foil and bake 45 minutes to 1 hour. Turn off the oven, open the oven door, and let the dish stand for about 10 minutes before serving.

Serves 6

BAKED ONION SOUP CASSEROLE

Onion soup lovers will crave this, too. When cooking onions for another recipe, why not cook these onions at the same time? Reserve the
cooked mixture for another time or bake the casserole for later reheating.

1 loaf French or Italian bread, cut into
   1-inch slices
4 tablespoons (½ stick) butter
6 large onions, sliced
4 garlic cloves, peeled and very finely
   chopped
1 teaspoon sugar (optional)
2 teaspoons soy sauce
Freshly ground black pepper

8 ounces Swiss cheese or a combination
   of Swiss and Parmesan, grated
Cooking spray
1 cup or 8-ounce can tomato puree
2 tablespoons tomato paste
12 cups fresh or canned chicken stock or
   broth
Salt

Preheat the oven to 300°F.

Place the slices of bread on the oven rack (not on a baking sheet) and bake
15 minutes, until crisp. Let cool on a wire rack.

Melt 2 tablespoons butter in each of 2 large skillets. Add the onions and
cook until soft and brown. After 15 minutes, add the garlic and continue cooking. Add ½ teaspoon sugar if using and 1 teaspoon soy sauce to each skillet
near the end of cooking. Season with lots of black pepper. ***This can be refrigerated for 24 hours.***

Cover each of the toasted bread slices (*croûtes*) with a layer of cheese about ¼
inch thick, reserving the remaining cheese. Spray a 5-quart Dutch oven with
cooking spray. Place a layer of cheese *croûtes* in the bottom of the pan. Top with
some of the remaining cheese. Cover with one-third of the browned onions.
Continue layering the onions and the *croûtes* until all are used, ending with
croûtes. Pat the remaining cheese over the top layer. Do not fill the casserole
more than two-thirds full, as the bread will swell as it cooks and absorbs liquid.

Whisk together the tomato-puree and tomato paste and add to one-half of
the stock.

Heat the tomato-stock mixture and ladle it into the pot until it comes halfway up the top layer of bread. Add salt and pepper to taste. Place in the oven and bake 1 to 1¼ hours, checking every 20 minutes and adding stock each time.

Serves 10 to 12

SESAME NOODLES WITH BROCCOLI

This tempting pasta dish is more filling than it appears and can serve as a main course as well as a side dish. If tahini paste is unavailable, try substituting peanut butter for a typically Thai flavor. This does not freeze but lasts several days in the refrigerator.

1 bunch broccoli, cut into florets
½ pound spaghetti
1 tablespoon chopped fresh ginger
2 garlic cloves, peeled and chopped
¼ cup tahini (sesame paste) or peanut butter

1 tablespoon sesame oil
1 tablespoon chili oil
¼ cup soy sauce
2 tablespoons rice wine vinegar
½ cup chopped cashews or almonds
4 green onions, chopped

Bring a large saucepan of water to the boil. Add the broccoli florets and blanch for about 1 minute. Remove the broccoli with a slotted spoon or strainer and refresh under cold water. Drain again and set aside. Add the spaghetti to the same boiling water and cook according to package directions, just until tender. Drain and set aside. *The broccoli and pasta can be covered and refrigerated separately for a day or 2.*

In a large bowl, combine the ginger, garlic, tahini, sesame oil, chili oil, soy sauce, and rice wine vinegar and blend thoroughly. Add the broccoli, pasta, and cashews and toss to coat evenly with the sauce. Refrigerate for at least 2 hours and up to 2 days before serving. Sprinkle with the green onions and serve at room temperature or slightly chilled.

Serves 6

PASTA WITH SWEET ONION SAUCE

This light but flavorful sauce is an easy approach to dressing up plain pasta. The sauce may be left to cook for up to an hour, giving you the time to prepare other parts of the meal, set the table, or relax a bit before serving. I have found that long pastas such as spaghetti, linguine, or fettuccine work best with this sauce, as they complement the "strands" of onion and Parmesan cheese.

3 tablespoons butter
3 tablespoons olive oil
12 medium yellow onions, thinly sliced
½ teaspoon salt
Freshly ground black pepper
1 cup dry white wine

¼ cup chopped fresh parsley
1 to 1½ pounds pasta, cooked and
drained
1 cup freshly grated imported Parmesan
cheese

Melt the butter and olive oil in a large sauté pan over low heat. Add the onions and salt, cover the pan, and cook over very low heat for about 1 hour, until the onions are meltingly soft. Uncover the pan and raise the heat to cook off any extra liquid. When the onions become golden, add several grinds of pepper and the white wine. Reduce the liquid by about two-thirds, stirring frequently, about 5 to 10 minutes. ***The sauce can be made and refrigerated a day or 2 in advance.***

Remove the pan from the heat, stir in the chopped parsley, and toss with the cooked drained pasta and the Parmesan cheese. Serve immediately.

Serves 6 to 8

Basic Vinaigrette ■ Celery Seed Dressing ■ Orange-Cumin
Vinaigrette ■ Cranberry Conserve ■ Cranberry-Jalapeño Chutney
■ American Tomato Salsa ■ Pineapple and Orange Salsa ■

ENHANCEMENTS

Horseradish Sauce ■ Pesto Sauce ■ Black Bean and Corn Salsa ■
Maître d'Hôtel Butter ■ Ginger-Shallot Butter ■ Herb Butter ■
Lemon and Lime Yogurt Sauce ■ Moroccan Preserved Lemons

IN AN EARLIER TIME the only things around to perk up simple cooked foods were bottled dressings and ketchup. No longer. We have entered the era of enhancements—those flavorful little extras that do so much to put a meal over the top. Whether freshly made or made ahead and preserved or stored in the freezer, they add a bit of punch to a meal, usually without any last-minute effort.

Salsa, the Spanish word for sauce, has replaced ketchup and chili sauce as a household staple. There is an endless variety of salsas, and you should consider those offered here merely as a starting point. The Black Bean and Corn Salsa is typical—it's an accommodating, easy-to-make friend that works just as successfully as a dip as it does as an accompaniment of meat, fish, or poultry.

Simply roasted meats and poultry, as well as plain blanched vegetables, can often use a dash of extra flavor, which is one reason I keep a variety of flavored butters and other enhancers in the freezer. A dab of herb butter makes a baked potato a meal, and a side dish of chutney accompanying a curry adds a glamorous touch. And should you have leftover cooked meats or vegetables, add some canned beans or greens, and you have an elegant salad that needs only a dose of zingy vinaigrette or other flavorful embellishment to make a lunch or light dinner.

BASIC VINAIGRETTE

This is a very simple vinaigrette that will keep in the refrigerator several weeks.

1 to 2 teaspoons Dijon mustard	*Salt*
¼ cup red wine vinegar	*Freshly ground black pepper*
¼ to ½ cup olive oil	*Sugar (optional)*
1 garlic clove, peeled and finely chopped	

In a small mixing bowl, whisk together the mustard and vinegar. Gradually whisk in the oil, then stir in the garlic, salt, and pepper. Taste for seasoning: If oily, add more salt; if still oily, add a pinch of sugar. For a thicker, more emulsified dressing, make it in a blender or food processor.

Makes ½ to ¾ cup

CELERY SEED DRESSING

This dressing is quite nice over a casual collection of lettuces. Store tightly covered in the refrigerator up to 2 weeks.

1 cup red wine vinegar	*1½ tablespoons sugar*
½ cup olive oil	*½ teaspoon paprika*
2 tablespoons Dijon mustard	*1 tablespoon celery seeds*

In a medium mixing bowl, whisk together the vinegar, olive oil, mustard, sugar, paprika, and celery seeds until well blended. For a smoother dressing, this may be emulsified in a food processor.

Makes 1¼ cups

ORANGE-CUMIN VINAIGRETTE

A wonderful alternative to a regular vinaigrette, this is excellent on a salad of bittersweet greens as well as a salad of fresh fruit. Try using it as a marinade for salmon fillets. It is enough for 4 to 6 fillets. Marinate overnight, then grill 10 minutes per inch of thickness.

1 tablespoon cumin seeds
2 tablespoons Dijon mustard
¼ cup balsamic vinegar
½ cup olive oil
3 garlic cloves, peeled and finely chopped

Grated peel (no white attached) and juice
of 1 orange
Salt
Freshly ground black pepper
Sugar (optional)

In a small, dry skillet, toast the cumin seeds over low heat until fragrant, 4 or 5 minutes. Let cool.

In a small mixing bowl, whisk together the mustard and vinegar. Gradually whisk in the oil, then stir in the garlic, orange peel and juice, and cumin seeds. Season to taste with salt and pepper. If the dressing tastes too oily, try adding more salt. If still oily, a small pinch of sugar will dispel it. For a thicker, more emulsified dressing, make it in a blender or food processor.

Makes ¾ cup

LEMON, LIME, OR ORANGE PEEL
Grate or zest lemons, limes, and oranges by rubbing the skin on a small hand grater, carefully avoiding any of the white; using one of the zesting gadgets now available; or peeling the skin with a potato peeler, scraping any white off the back, and chop. Store, tightly covered, up to one week in the refrigerator, or freeze.

CRANBERRY CONSERVE

We always try to keep this conserve on hand throughout the holidays. It is an excellent condiment for the holiday turkey or a simple pork tenderloin. Be sure to use a plastic spoon when stirring; a wooden spoon will absorb the cranberry color. This can also be mixed with cream cheese and left-over chopped turkey and spooned into little phyllo baskets (page 55) for a quick and easy cocktail munchie. It can be stored in the refrigerator for 1 to 2 months, and freezes 2 to 3 months.

1 pound cranberries (about 4 cups)
1½ cups orange juice
3 cups sugar
1 cup crushed pineapple, drained

½ cup raisins or currants
2 oranges, peeled, seeded, and cut into
   wedges or sections
½ cup walnuts, chopped

Combine the cranberries and orange juice in a heavy 3-quart saucepan. Bring to the boil over moderately high heat and cook 6 to 8 minutes, or until the berries begin to pop and are tender. Stir in the sugar, pineapple, raisins, and oranges, reduce heat to low, and simmer uncovered, stirring occasionally for 1 hour, or until thick and jam-like. Stir in the walnuts. Store in the refrigerator or freeze.

CRANBERRY-JALAPEÑO CHUTNEY

It's amazing how this chutney can perk up a plain roast and convince everyone you've gone to a lot of trouble. And, of course, curries love chutney. This spicy sweet blend makes a wonderful holiday gift; stir it together while you are waiting for fruitcakes to come out of the oven. I keep my chutney in the refrigerator as I like it cold and ready. It's so cooling I think of it year-round.

5 cups tart apples, peeled and thinly
  sliced
2 cups light brown sugar
1½ cups cider vinegar
½ cup thinly sliced crystallized ginger
2 onions, thinly sliced
1 cup golden raisins
3 cups cranberries, washed and picked
  over

4 to 6 jalapeño peppers, seeded and finely chopped
1 tablespoon mustard seeds
1 teaspoon salt
1 teaspoon pepper
1 cup sliced almonds

In a large stockpot over medium heat, combine the apples, brown sugar, cider vinegar, ginger, onions, raisins, cranberries, jalapeño peppers, mustard seeds, salt, and pepper. Bring to the boil over medium heat, then reduce the heat and simmer, uncovered, for about 30 to 45 minutes, or until thick, stirring occasionally to prevent scorching. Stir in the almonds. Pour the boiling mixture into sterilized jars leaving ⅛ inch of the top; wipe the rims and seal at once. Optimally, wait 4 weeks before eating to let the flavors mingle, but it may be eaten at once. Serve with pork, chicken, ham, or turkey.

Makes eight 4-ounce jars

AMERICAN TOMATO SALSA

This was invented here in America by Pierre-Henri, using his memory of Morocco and his famous preserved lemon peel, which transports an old standby to another realm of creativity.

The salsa is like a conserve or condiment, ready to be served alongside a stew, on top of vegetables, or as a dip smeared on a piece of bread. It keeps several days in the refrigerator and also freezes for up to 6 months.

4 pounds ripe tomatoes
¼ cup peanut or olive oil
½ tablespoon salt
1½ tablespoons paprika
1 garlic clove, peeled and crushed
1 green or red bell pepper, seeded and
    chopped

2 to 3 small hot peppers, finely chopped
1 preserved (page 158) or fresh lemon
    peel, finely chopped
1 cup chopped fresh parsley

Peel and seed the tomatoes and cut them in large pieces. Heat the oil in a large pot and add the tomatoes, salt, paprika, and garlic. Bring to the boil, reduce the heat, and simmer, stirring frequently, until the liquid has evaporated. When you see oil on top of the tomatoes, add the chopped bell pepper, hot peppers, lemon peel, and parsley. Let it simmer 15 minutes, stirring occasionally. It can be eaten hot or cold.

Makes 6 cups

PINEAPPLE AND ORANGE SALSA

This tasty salsa goes especially well with Duck with Orange and Mint (page 104). It has a nice, sweet fruit taste with just a little zip to it with the added mint. The salsa will give a nice contrast to your entrée. Store tightly covered in the refrigerator for up to a week.

1 20-ounce can crushed pineapple in
   juice, drained, juice reserved
¼ cup packed light brown sugar
2 tablespoons orange juice
1 tablespoon arrowroot

1 11-ounce can mandarin oranges,
   drained
4 sprigs of finely sliced mint leaves
Pinch of salt
Whole mint leaves for garnish (optional)

In a saucepan, heat the pineapple juice, brown sugar, orange juice, and arrowroot for 3 to 5 minutes. The mixture should begin to thicken. Add the pineapple, oranges, mint leaves, and salt. Simmer 5 to 6 minutes. Remove from heat and cool. Garnish with whole mint leaves if using.

Makes 2 cups

HORSERADISH SAUCE

I really love the zip of this sauce. It goes well with beef, such as tenderloin or the standing rib roast (page 60), and is nice on asparagus and sandwiches. Store, covered, in the refrigerator up to 2 weeks.

2 cups mayonnaise
⅔ cup prepared horseradish

1½ teaspoons Worcestershire sauce

In a small bowl, whisk together the mayonnaise, horseradish, and Worcestershire sauce until well blended.

Makes 2½ cups

PESTO SAUCE

I often wonder where I would be without pesto sauce. I always have it on hand to spoon over pasta, chicken, rice, beef—its uses are endless. And it freezes for up to 6 months!

6 to 8 garlic cloves, peeled and chopped
4 cups fresh basil leaves, packed tightly
½ to 1 cup imported olive oil

2 to 3 cups freshly grated imported
  Parmesan cheese
¼ cup pine nuts (optional)

Place the garlic, basil leaves, olive oil, cheese, and pine nuts if using in a food processor or blender and process until pureed. It will keep several weeks, refrigerated.

Makes 3 cups

BLACK BEAN AND CORN SALSA

S alsas are the chili sauces of the decade. They complement a vast array of meats, poultry, and fish, and can even be served with vegetables or chips as a dip. This one is full of vim—crunchy and mildly spicy.

1 15-ounce can black beans, drained and
  rinsed
2 ears corn, cooked and cut off the cob
1 large ripe tomato, peeled, seeded, and
  chopped

¼ cup finely chopped onion
1 jalapeño pepper, seeded and chopped
¼ cup lemon or lime juice
2 tablespoons finely chopped fresh
  cilantro

Mix the beans, corn, tomato, onion, pepper, lemon juice, and cilantro together in a bowl. Chill until ready to serve.

Makes 2½ cups

MAITRE D'HOTEL BUTTER

A slice of this herb butter is delicious on broiled steak, fish, or vegetables. A truly multipurpose addition, it freezes for 2 to 3 months. Lightly cream the butter. Stir in the salt, pepper, parsley, and lemon juice.

½ cup (1 stick) unsalted butter, at room
    temperature
1 teaspoon salt

¼ teaspoon white pepper
2 teaspoons finely chopped fresh parsley
3 tablespoons fresh lemon juice

Put the butter mixture on a piece of wax paper. Form the butter into a cylinder 4½ to 5 inches long. Chill or freeze.

Makes ½ cup

GINGER-SHALLOT BUTTER

D elicious melted over corn on the cob or other freshly steamed vegetables, this butter also makes a nice basting sauce for fish or chicken on the grill. If you like, substitute balsamic vinegar for the sherry. It freezes well for 2 to 3 months.

1 cup (2 sticks) butter, softened
2 shallots, chopped
3 tablespoons sherry
2 tablespoons chopped fresh ginger

1 tablespoon chopped fresh chives
1 tablespoon chopped fresh cilantro
4 green onions, white part only, chopped
2 teaspoons paprika

In a small skillet, melt 3 tablespoons of the butter. Add the shallots and cook until a nice golden brown, about 5 to 6 minutes. Add the sherry and simmer until the liquid has evaporated, then set aside to cool. In a bowl, combine the shallot mixture, the remaining butter, ginger, chives, cilantro, green onions, and paprika. Mix well and chill or freeze until ready to use.

Makes 1¼ cups

CLARIFIED BUTTER
Clarified butter is simply melted butter with the milk solids and salt removed. I usually melt the butter several hours or days ahead of time and refrigerate it, making it easy to remove the top and bottom layers. Because the milk solids have been removed, clarified butter can take a higher heat without burning.

To clarify butter, melt 2 sticks over low heat. Remove from the heat and let stand several minutes until the milk solids settle to the bottom. Spoon or pour off the clear liquid and discard the bottom layer of milk solids. *Makes ¾ cup*

HERB BUTTER

Herb butter is a wonderful accompaniment for a variety of dishes. Try it with asparagus, broiled meats, or fillet of fish. Use unsalted butter to allow the herb flavor to come through. You may add a touch of white wine for a kick.

½ cup (1 stick) unsalted butter, at room temperature

¼ cup finely chopped fresh herbs, such as tarragon or basil

Cream the butter slightly and stir in the herbs. Put the butter mixture on a piece of wax paper. Form the butter into a log 4½ to 5 inches long. Chill or freeze.

Makes ½ cup

LEMON AND LIME YOGURT SAUCE

We are always finding something new this sauce complements, but it's particularly good with the Summer Fruit Fantasy (page 175).

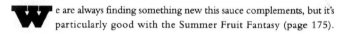

1 cup plain lowfat yogurt
3 tablespoons lemon juice
2 tablespoons lime juice
Chopped peel (no white attached) of 1 lemon

Chopped peel (no white attached) of 1 lime
¼ cup confectioners' sugar
½ teaspoon almond extract

In a small bowl, whisk together the yogurt, lemon juice, lime juice, lemon peel, lime peel, confectioners' sugar, and almond extract.

Makes 1 cup

MOROCCAN PRESERVED LEMONS

My son-in-law Pierre-Henri is an enthusiastic cook, with an excellent palate, no doubt educated by his mother, Jozette. She was a talented home cook long before she took lessons at the Ritz Hotel in Paris. She and Pierre-Henri's father lived in Morocco when Pierre-Henri was a boy and passed along a love of this cuisine to him. Not long after he and Audrey came to stay with me, he put up a batch of these Moroccan preserved lemons. The large yellow ovals in a tall glass jar were incredibly alluring on the kitchen counter. Everyone asked what they were. Everyone wanted to taste them. After a month of torturous waiting, he dazzled us with several recipes. I've since devised many other ways to use them. Only the rind of these lemons is used; it is not as sharp as the rind of fresh lemons. A word of warning: An unattractive scum from the lemons may rise to the top. It is not dangerous and may be skimmed off and discarded.

LEMON, LIME, OR ORANGE PEEL
Grate or zest lemons, limes, and oranges by rubbing the skin on a small hand grater, carefully avoiding any of the white; using one of the zesting gadgets now available; or peeling the skin with a potato peeler, scraping any white off the back, and chop. Store, tightly covered, up to one week in the refrigerator, or freeze.

14 large lemons   *9 tablespoons salt*

Wash the lemons, scrubbing them if necessary to remove any stamps or markings. Cut each lemon vertically from the stem nearly to the blossom end, keeping the halves joined. Salt the exposed surface of each lemon with at least 1 teaspoon of salt.

Fill a container with the lemons with as little excess space as possible. Cover the lemons with lukewarm water mixed with the remaining salt and top with a clean stone or weight (not marble or limestone) to keep all the lemons immersed. Cover tightly and let sit 1 month before using. To use, remove the yellow part of the rind, and discard the lemon flesh and pith. The rind can then be sectioned, sliced, or chopped.

Makes 14

Nearly French Bread ■ *Challah* ■ *Garlic-Thyme Corn Muffins*
■ *Country Ham and Cheese Bread* ■ *Chocolate Chunk Bread* ■
Dark Bread with Nuts and Raisins ■ *Onion-Walnut Bread*

BREADS

■ *Ray's Roasted Pepper-Onion Bread* ■ *Sour Cream and Chive*
Bread ■ *Whole Wheat Olive Bread* ■ *Cumin Party Biscuits*
■ *Sweet and Spicy Squash Muffins*

THE VALUE of making bread lies not just in the sustenance the bread itself provides. Homemade bread is the crowning touch of any meal, bringing warmth and pleasure not only to the stomach but to the heart as well. It's especially welcome when everyone is eating at a different time—just heat up the soup and slice the bread. I make bread or rolls nearly every day when my schedule permits.

It may sound ironic to say that I think of making bread when I am too busy to grocery shop for it, but in reality baking a loaf takes less of my actual time than getting in the car, going to the store, checking out, and driving home! When there is washing and ironing to be done it is the ideal time to pull out the flour and yeast and start the bread. And nothing compares to the aroma of bread baking.

The *total* amount of time it takes to make a yeast bread includes mixing and kneading (which I usually do in the food processor), rising, shaping, a second rising, and baking. In actual hands-on time, it takes less than fifteen minutes for a week's worth of bread. If it's necessary to speed up the process, rapid-rise yeast (which eliminates one rising) and rising in the microwave are added time-savers.

Sometimes I'll start a batch of bread while I'm waiting for supper to finish cooking, then I'll knead it and leave it to rise overnight (or even several days) in the refrigerator. Once I have some time home again, I pull it out, shape it, let it rise, and bake it. Either way, fresh baked bread (or even reheated frozen) creates an instant aura of welcome.

NEARLY FRENCH BREAD

I love crisp French bread like those made in a wood-burning fire in French bakeries—so crisp on the outside it cracks, with tender, soft dough inside. These long, thin loaves run a close second to that bread. Setting a pan of water on the bottom of the oven helps give the bread its crisp crust. Like one-day-old traditional French bread, these loaves can be refreshed by sprinkling quickly with water and reheating in a 400°F. oven. They freeze for up to 3 months.

2 packages active dry yeast
1½ tablespoons sugar
1 cup warm water (105°F. to 115°F.)
3 to 4 cups bread flour
1 teaspoon salt

1 tablespoon cornmeal

G L A Z E
1 egg, beaten with 1 tablespoon water

Dissolve the yeast and sugar in the warm water. In a food processor, by hand, or in a mixer, combine 2½ cups of the flour, the salt, and the yeast mixture. Process or knead, adding more of the remaining flour as needed, until the dough is elastic and smooth as a baby's bottom, allowing 1 minute in a food processor or 5 to 10 minutes by hand or in a mixer. Place in an oiled plastic bag or oiled bowl and turn to coat. Seal or cover and let rise until doubled, about 1 hour. Punch down. Shape into 2 long loaves. Place on a baking sheet sprinkled with the cornmeal and let double again, about 45 minutes.

Preheat the oven to 400°F. Brush the loaves with the egg glaze and slash the tops with a sharp knife. Place on the middle rack of the oven with a small cake pan of boiling water on the bottom rack. Bake 20 to 25 minutes, until crisp and the bottoms sound hollow when tapped. Cool on racks.

Makes 2 loaves

CHALLAH

This light, rich bread is wonderful by itself or spread with warm honey. The double braid is very easy to accomplish and yields a most impressive result. The friend who gave me the recipe explains that oil is used in accordance with Orthodox Jewish tradition since butter can not be eaten at certain meals. Double the recipe and make one to freeze. It freezes up to 3 months.

2 packages active dry yeast
2 teaspoons sugar
1 cup warm water (105°F. to 115°F.)
4 to 5 cups bread flour
2 teaspoons salt
3 eggs
½ cup vegetable oil or butter

G L A Z E
1 egg
1 tablespoon water

Poppy seeds, sesame seeds, or kosher salt

YEAST
Active and rapid-rise yeasts are interchangeable in all important ways, although they are different strains of yeast, with different flavors. Active yeast granules, however, are larger and need to be dissolved in liquid or they may not incorporate into the dough the same way. It is not really necessary to "proof" yeast, whether active or rapid rise, unless the expiration date on the package has passed.

In a small bowl or measuring cup, dissolve the yeast and sugar in the warm water. In a large bowl or food processor, mix together 3½ cups of the flour and the salt. Add the yeast mixture, then the eggs, oil, and enough flour to make a thick dough. Continue adding flour ½ cup at a time, kneading on a floured board or in an electric mixer about 5 to 10 minutes or about 1 minute in the processor until the dough is elastic and smooth as a baby's bottom. Place the dough in an oiled bag or bowl, seal or cover with plastic wrap, and let rise 1 hour.

Remove the dough, punch it down, and cut off about one-third of the dough, leaving two-thirds of the dough in one piece. Divide each piece into thirds (you now have 6 pieces of dough). Roll the pieces into ropes about 14 to 16 inches long. Braid the 3 larger dough ropes together, pinch the ends together, and place the braid on a lightly greased baking sheet. Repeat the process with the remaining dough, making a smaller braid, and place it on top of the first braid. Pinch all the ends to keep the 2 braids joined. Let rise until doubled, about 45 minutes.

Preheat the oven to 375°F. Mix together the egg and water and brush the braided dough with the glaze. Sprinkle with seeds or salt if desired. Bake 15 minutes, then reduce the heat to 350°F. and bake 35 to 40 minutes longer, or until the loaf is golden and sounds hollow when tapped. Cover the bread with foil if it begins to brown too quickly. Remove the pan from the oven and place on a wire rack about 5 minutes, then remove the bread from the pan and continue cooling on the rack.

Makes 1 large loaf

GARLIC-THYME CORN MUFFINS

 fter you've gotten everything else in the oven, take a few quick moments to fix these extra-special muffins.

1¼ cups cornmeal	1 teaspoon garlic powder
¾ cup all-purpose flour	1 tablespoon chopped fresh thyme or
1 tablespoon sugar	1 teaspoon dried thyme
1 tablespoon plus 1 teaspoon baking	2 large eggs, lightly beaten
powder	1 cup milk
¾ teaspoon salt	¼ cup vegetable oil

Preheat the oven to 425°F. Grease a 12-cup muffin tin.

In a large bowl, combine the cornmeal, flour, sugar, baking powder, salt, garlic powder, and thyme. Mix thoroughly and make a well in the center of the mixture. In a mixing cup combine the eggs, milk, and oil; add to the dry ingredients, stirring just until moistened. Spoon the batter into the muffin tin, filling two-thirds full. Bake until lightly browned, 15 to 20 minutes.

Makes 1 dozen

COUNTRY HAM AND
CHEESE BREAD

Served with a nice vegetable soup and fresh fruit for dessert, this savory, hearty bread rounds out a menu perfectly. I make it ahead and freeze it, saving it for days when I don't have the time or energy to pull together a substantial meal. The dough can also be shaped into egg-size rolls, allowed to double, and then baked for 25 minutes, or until golden brown. It freezes for up to 3 months.

1 cup warm water (105°F. to 115°F.)
1 tablespoon sugar
2 packages active dry yeast
3½ to 4½ cups bread flour
1 teaspoon salt
½ teaspoon black pepper
2 eggs

¼ cup olive oil
1 cup grated Cheddar cheese
2 cups minced country ham, blanched for
*   2 minutes, drained, and patted dry, or*
*   boiled ham or salami*
Cornmeal, for dusting

In a small bowl, mix together the water, sugar, and yeast. In a large bowl or food processor, combine 3 cups of the flour, the salt, pepper, eggs, and olive oil. Add the yeast mixture and enough of the flour, ½ cup at a time, to make a soft dough. Knead by hand or in a food processor until the dough is smooth and elastic, about 10 minutes by hand or mixer or 1 minute in the processor. Add more flour if necessary. Place in an oiled bowl or zip-type bag and let double in volume, about 1 hour. Punch down and knead in the cheese and ham. Shape into 2 oblong loaves and place on a greased baking sheet that has been dusted with cornmeal. Let double in a warm place, about 1 hour.

Preheat the oven to 375°F. Slash the top of each loaf with a sharp knife and bake about 40 minutes, or until golden brown. Remove to a wire rack and cool.

Makes 2 loaves

CHOCOLATE CHUNK BREAD

I do love a cup of tea midafternoon and every once in a while I indulge myself with a dessert bread or sweet. One day I had a craving for chocolate bread. Once this was ready I put my feet up and ate it slathered with chocolate butter as I listened to some music and drank my tea.

This bread freezes well for up to 3 months. It is hard to decide whether the defrosted bread is better at room temperature—soft and tender—or slightly warmed so the chocolate is melting and smooth.

2 packages active dry yeast	½ teaspoon salt
¼ cup sugar	2½ to 3½ cups bread flour
½ cup warm water (105°F. to 115°F.)	5 ounces semisweet chocolate mini-morsels
½ cup semisweet chocolate chips	morsels
½ cup warm milk (105°F. to 115°F.)	
1 tablespoon plus 1 teaspoon cocoa	Chocolate Butter (see sidebar, left)

Dissolve the yeast and sugar in the warm water in a medium-size bowl. Melt the chocolate chips in a microwave or over low heat. Cool slightly, then stir in the warm milk and add to the yeast.

Mix together the cocoa, salt, and 2½ cups of the flour in a large mixing bowl or food processor. Add the yeast mixture. Knead by hand or food processor, adding flour as necessary. Knead until the dough is smooth and elastic, about 1 minute in the processor or 10 minutes by hand or in the mixer. Knead in the chocolate morsels. Put in an oiled bowl or plastic bag, cover or seal, and place in a warm area to rise for 1½ hours.

Punch down and put in a buttered 9 × 5 × 3-inch loaf pan. Let the dough rise again for about 1 hour, or until it reaches over the top of the pan.

Preheat the oven to 350°F. Bake the bread for 50 minutes, or until a toothpick comes out clean. Cover with foil if the bread begins to brown too quickly. Turn out onto a rack and let cool completely before cutting. Serve with the chocolate butter.

Makes 1 loaf

DARK BREAD WITH NUTS
AND RAISINS

This bread is chock-full of luscious raisins and whole nuts with only a minimal amount of dough holding it all together. The chocolate and cocoa make it a deep, rich brown, with full flavor and texture. Plumped raisins always seem to work better than nonplumped ones in a yeast bread. If you want a darker bread, heat ¼ cup of the liquid from the raisins instead of plain water. Bake 2 loaves and give one to a friend. The bread freezes for up to 3 months.

2 packages active dry yeast	½ teaspoon salt
2 teaspoons sugar	½ cup cocoa
¼ cup warm water (105°F. to 115°F.)	1 cup chopped pecans
¼ cup molasses	1 cup whole pecans
½ cup milk	1½ cups dark and golden raisins,
¼ cup butter	plumped overnight in hot water and
1 ounce unsweetened chocolate	drained
2 to 3 cups bread flour	

Preheat the oven to 350°F. Grease a baking sheet.

In a small bowl, dissolve the yeast and sugar in the warm water. In a small saucepan over low heat, mix together the molasses, milk, butter, and chocolate until the chocolate melts. In a food processor, mix together 2 cups of the flour, the salt, and the cocoa. Add the yeast mixture and then the molasses mixture and process until smooth. Add the remaining flour a little at a time until you have a very smooth and elastic dough. Place in an oiled bag or bowl and seal or cover with plastic wrap. This bread is too heavy to double, but let sit for 2 hours. Punch down and knead in the nuts and raisins by hand until they are evenly distributed. Shape the dough into a round or oval and place on a baking sheet to double again, about 1 hour. Place a small pan of hot water on the lowest rack and bake the bread on the middle rack of the oven about 45 to 50 minutes, until the bread sounds hollow when tapped on the bottom. Remove from the oven and let cool on a wire rack.

Makes 1 loaf

GREAT MEALS FOR BUSY DAYS

**MICROWAVE
AND YEAST
DOUGHS**
To speed up bread making, try "microwave rising": Form the dough into a ball. With your thumbs, punch a hole to form a doughnut shape and place into the bowl of your food processor without the blade. Cover loosely with a damp tea towel or plastic wrap. Place in the microwave.

Place an 8-ounce glass of water in the back of the microwave. (This lowers the "heat" in the oven to avoid killing the yeast.) Lower the microwave power to 10% or the next to lowest power setting. Heat for 3 minutes. Rest for 3 minutes. Repeat heating for 3 minutes and resting for 3 minutes. Repeat for third time by heating 3 minutes and resting 6 minutes until the dough has doubled in bulk.

ONION-WALNUT BREAD

Hearty and healthy, this dense bread is a good accompaniment to a soup and salad meal, every bite seeming to have a different flavor. My students voted this their favorite. I find it's better to knead by hand, but the flours, bran, and yeast can be mixed in the food processor, and you can add the onions and walnuts by hand or process the nuts and onions right into the flour. It freezes well for 2 to 3 months.

2 packages active dry yeast	*1 cup whole wheat flour*
1 teaspoon sugar	*2 teaspoons salt*
1½ cups warm water (105°F. to	*¼ cup all-bran cereal*
115°F.)	*½ cup rye flour*
1 tablespoon butter or olive oil	*½ cup chopped walnuts*
½ cup chopped onion	*2 to 3 cups bread flour*

Dissolve the yeast and sugar in ½ cup of the warm water. Heat the oil in a small skillet. Add the onion and sauté over medium heat until softened, 5 minutes. Set aside.

In a large mixing bowl, combine the whole wheat flour, salt, bran cereal, rye flour, onion, and walnuts. Mix thoroughly. Add the remaining cup of warm water to the yeast mixture and add to the mixing bowl. Stir to mix well. Stir in the bread flour, ½ cup at a time, to make a smooth dough.

Turn out onto a floured board and knead until elastic and smooth as a baby's bottom. Place in an oiled plastic bag or oiled bowl, seal or cover, and let rise until doubled, about 1 hour. Punch down, shape into a round, and place on a greased baking sheet. Cover with a tea towel and let rise until doubled again, about 45 minutes.

Preheat the oven to 375°F. Bake 45 to 50 minutes, or until a toothpick inserted in the center comes out clean. Cool on a rack.

Makes 1 loaf

RAY'S ROASTED PEPPER-ONION BREAD

This is a delightful peasant bread with delicious taste, texture, and color and a subtle Mediterranean flair. Omit the olives for a variation. It freezes well for 2 to 3 months.

2 packages active dry yeast
2 teaspoons sugar
1 cup warm water (105°F. to 115°F.)
1 to 2 teaspoons salt
5 tablespoons olive oil
1 tablespoon butter
3 onions, sliced
2 red peppers, roasted, peeled, seeded, and chopped

2 tablespoons chopped fresh rosemary
2 teaspoons cracked black pepper
4 to 5 cups bread flour
¾ cup chopped black olives
Cornmeal, for sprinkling

GLAZE
1 egg, beaten with 1 tablespoon water

YEAST BREADS AND THE FOOD PROCESSOR
I almost always combine and knead doughs in the food processor. First, place the bread or steel knife blade in the bottom of the bowl. (I see very little difference in the result of the two blades and tend to use the steel knife as it is the one I keep out.) Place the dry ingredients in the bowl, then add the liquid. Process ("knead") one minute, then test the dough to see if it bounces back.
The dough may now be doubled in a plastic bag or oiled bowl set in a warm (not hot) place, which takes approximately an hour.

In a large bowl, dissolve the yeast and sugar in the warm water. Add the salt and olive oil to the yeast mixture.

Meanwhile, heat the butter in a skillet. Add the onions and sauté over medium heat until soft, 4 or 5 minutes. Remove from the heat and add the red peppers, rosemary, and cracked pepper.

Add 4 cups of the flour to the yeast and mix until a soft dough forms. Add the onion-red pepper mixture and the olives. Knead by hand or in an electric mixer, adding more flour as needed, until the dough is elastic and smooth as a baby's bottom. Place in an oiled plastic bag or oiled bowl, seal or cover, and let rise until doubled, about 1 hour. Punch down the dough and divide it into 2 pieces. Shape each piece into a 12-inch oblong. Place them on an oiled cookie sheet sprinkled with cornmeal and allow to double again, about 30 to 45 minutes.

Preheat the oven to 375°F. Brush the loaves with the egg glaze and slash the tops with a sharp knife. Bake 25 to 30 minutes, until golden brown and the bottoms sound hollow when tapped. Cool on a rack.

Makes 2 loaves

SOUR CREAM AND CHIVE BREAD

If you like your baked potato with sour cream and chives, wait until you
try this bread. It has a wonderful texture with just the right amount of
subtle flavor so as not to overpower whatever it is served with. If chives are
unavailable, finely chopped green onions will make a nice substitute. It freezes
for 2 to 3 months.

1 package active dry yeast	3 tablespoons olive oil
1 tablespoon sugar	1 egg
¼ cup warm water (105°F. to 115°F.)	⅔ cup sour cream
2½ to 3½ cups bread flour	2 tablespoons chopped fresh chives
1 teaspoon salt	2 tablespoons milk
1 teaspoon pepper	

In a small bowl, dissolve the yeast and sugar in the water. In a food processor, combine 2½ cups of the flour, salt, pepper, olive oil, egg, sour cream, and
chives. Process to blend, then add the yeast mixture and combine. Knead until
the dough is elastic and smooth as a baby's bottom, adding more flour ½ cup
at a time as needed. Place the dough in an oiled plastic bag or bowl, seal or
cover with plastic wrap, and let double, about 1 hour. When doubled, punch
down the dough and shape into 2 rounds. Place on a greased baking sheet. Let
double again, about 45 minutes.

Preheat the oven to 375°F. With a knife, score the top of each dough round
in a tic-tac-toe pattern. Brush with the milk and bake 40 to 45 minutes, or
until the bread is deep brown and the bottoms sound hollow when tapped.
Remove from the oven and place the bread on wire racks to cool.

Makes 2 loaves

WHOLE WHEAT OLIVE BREAD

Chock-full of olives and onions, this is a hearty bread, good on its own or as a base for a ham sandwich. It freezes up to 3 months.

¼ cup olive oil
1 cup finely chopped onion
2 packages active dry yeast
1¼ cups warm water (105°F. to
    115°F.)
1 teaspoon honey

1 teaspoon salt
1 cup coarsely chopped black olives,
    preferably Greek or Spanish
2 tablespoons finely chopped fresh thyme
2½ cups whole wheat flour
1½ to 2 cups bread flour

**STORING
YEAST
DOUGHS**
Any yeast bread dough
can be kept, covered
and refrigerated, before
shaping and baking, for
up to 24 hours. Some
may be kept longer if it
is a dense, not delicate,
dough. It is then
shaped, doubled, and
baked as usual.

In a medium skillet, heat the olive oil, add the onion, and cook until soft, 4 or 5 minutes. Set aside to cool.

Dissolve the yeast in the water with the honey. In a medium mixing bowl, combine the yeast mixture, onion mixture, salt, olives, and thyme and stir well. Add the whole wheat flour and stir to combine well. Add enough of the bread flour, ½ cup at a time, to make a stiff dough. Turn out onto a floured surface and knead until smooth and elastic, adding flour as necessary. Place in an oiled bowl, cover with plastic wrap or in a plastic bag, and set aside to rise until doubled in bulk, about 1 hour.

Punch down and divide the dough in half. Shape into 2 round loaves, flatten them slightly, and place them on an oiled baking sheet. Set aside to rise again until doubled.

Preheat the oven to 375°F. Bake 35 to 45 minutes, or until well browned and the loaves sound hollow when tapped on the bottom. Cool on racks.

Makes 2 small loaves

CUMIN PARTY BISCUITS

Entertaining is so much easier when these biscuits are made and in the freezer. Whether split and filled with ham or turkey or served on their own, they'll bring raves from your guests. They freeze for up to 3 months.

2½ cups self-rising soft wheat flour, plus extra for flouring the board
½ teaspoon salt
2 tablespoons cumin seeds, lightly toasted and crushed (page 98)

Grated peel (no white attached) of 1 lemon
¼ cup shortening
1 cup buttermilk

Preheat the oven to 500° F. Lightly grease a baking sheet.

Sift the flour and salt together in a medium mixing bowl. Add the cumin seeds and lemon peel. Cut in the shortening until the mixture resembles coarse meal. Make a well in the center, add the buttermilk all at once, and mix gently with a fork until the dough holds together. Do not overwork the dough; it should be wet, sticky, and lumpy.

Turn the the dough out onto a generously floured surface. Cover with more flour and pat gently out into a round about ½ to ¾ inch thick. Cut into rounds with a 1½-inch cutter. Place on the baking sheet with the sides touching each other. Bake until golden, about 10 to 12 minutes. Transfer to a wire rack to cool.

Makes about 36 1½-inch biscuits

SWEET AND SPICY
SQUASH MUFFINS

This quick, easy, and tasty muffin is really a snap to make. The sweetness is balanced nicely with the spices, and the addition of the vegetables and chopped almonds offers a nice texture. These are even better when allowed to sit overnight, giving the flavors a chance to marry. They freeze for up to 3 months.

1 yellow summer squash, shredded and squeezed dry	*¼ cup vegetable oil*
1 zucchini, shredded and squeezed dry	*1¾ cups self-rising flour*
Grated peel (no white attached) of 2 lemons or oranges	*½ teaspoon salt*
	1 teaspoon ground cinnamon
	1 teaspoon ground coriander
½ cup chopped almonds	*½ teaspoon mace*
2 large eggs, beaten to mix	*½ teaspoon freshly grated nutmeg*

Preheat the oven to 350°F. Grease and flour a 12-cup muffin tin or lightly spray with a nonstick vegetable spray. Set aside.

In a large bowl, mix together the squash, zucchini, lemon or orange peel, almonds, eggs, and vegetable oil. In another bowl, sift together the flour, salt, cinnamon, coriander, mace, and nutmeg. Add the flour mixture to the liquid mixture and stir until just combined. Fill each muffin cup about three-quarters full. Bake the muffins 25 to 30 minutes, or until a skewer inserted into the center comes out clean. Remove from the oven, tip out onto a wire rack, and let cool before serving.

Makes 12

Summer Fruit Fantasy ■ Pear and Apple Phyllo Triangles ■ Christmas
Coffee Cake ■ Abby's Pecan Applecake ■ Cranberry Crisp ■ Heath Bar
Cheesecake ■ Low-Cal Ricotta Cheesecake ■ White Chocolate
Cheesecake ■ Meringues ■ Dacquoises ■ Raspberry Meringue Cake ■
Choco-Mint Boule de Neige ■ Chocolate Shards ■ Italian Biscotti ■

DESSERTS

Grandmother Kreiser's Icebox Cookies ■ Summer Pudding ■ Oranges with
Ginger Custard ■ Ginger-Apricot Flan ■ Indestructible Baked Lemon
Soufflé Pudding ■ Marbled Chocolate Mousse ■ Grape and Apricot Tart
■ Amethyst Pie ■ Markham Family Lemon Meringue Pie ■ Plum Pie ■
Browned Butter Tart Pastry ■ Perfect Piecrust ■ All-Fruit Cobbler

I'M CONSTANTLY promising myself that I'll give up desserts, but so far I haven't been successful. Even on the busiest of days I find myself wanting to eat—or serve—something sweet. But in order to truly enjoy these indulgences I have found it best to make desserts when there is some time, so that they do not become last-minute affairs that take me away from my friends or guests just as dinner swings into high gear.

Fortunately, a great many desserts (with the exception of some fresh fruit desserts) can be made well ahead, or else prepared and left to bake or chill while the main course is being eaten. Many cakes and baked goods whip together in a snap, needing only a long, slow baking time. Cheesecakes can be made up to several days ahead and refrigerated or even frozen.

Another option is to assemble a dessert from partially premade components, such as piecrusts you've mixed, rolled, and then frozen. With ready-to-go piecrusts, Amethyst Pie or Markham Family Lemon Meringue Pie are fabulous and easy additions to any meal.

Meringues are another great convenience to keep in the freezer, and take very little "people time" to prepare if you are willing to be patient and allow them to dry thoroughly in the oven to cloudlike perfection. Cookies too can be stored in the freezer, both in their unbaked dough form (fun to have for a quick cooking project with the kids) or baked and stored in sturdy containers.

SUMMER FRUIT FANTASY

Ray threw this light dessert together one summer day when all the fruit was at its peak. It was heavenly, cooling, and memorable. I long for it on hot days. Try it as a starter without the yogurt sauce. This can be refrigerated for 2 days.

1 cantaloupe, peeled, seeded, and cut
    into 1-inch chunks
5 peaches, peeled, pitted, and sliced
¾ cup cherries, pitted and halved
1 to 3 teaspoons sugar, depending on
    sweetness of the fruit

3 to 4 tablespoons chopped lemon balm
    or mint
Lemon and Lime Yogurt sauce
    (page 157)

In a large bowl, toss together the cantaloupe, peaches, cherries, strawberries, sugar, and lemon balm. Chill for at least 1 hour for flavors to marry. Serve with Lemon and Lime Yogurt Sauce, if desired.

Serves 8 to 10

N O T E : *Other fruits you might add include 1 cup blueberries, 3 plums, pitted and sliced, 1 cup pineapple chunks, 2 bananas, sliced.*

PEAR AND APPLE PHYLLO
TRIANGLES

Crisp, buttery phyllo pastry is an excellent way to dress up simple ingredients. These filled pastries may be frozen or made ahead a couple of days and kept refrigerated, then reheated at will. They can be frozen up to 6 months.

2 tablespoons butter

1 large or 2 small Granny Smith apples,
  peeled, seeded, and chopped

1 large pear, peeled, seeded, and chopped

2 tablespoons packed brown sugar (light
  or dark)

⅛ teaspoon freshly grated nutmeg

¼ teaspoon ground cinnamon

2 to 3 teaspoons finely chopped orange
  peel (no white attached)

½ cup chopped walnuts

6 14 × 18-inch sheets phyllo pastry

½ cup Clarified Butter (see sidebar,
  page 156)

Preheat the oven to 400° F.

Melt the butter in a large skillet. Add the apples and sauté over medium heat for 2 to 3 minutes. Add the pear, brown sugar, nutmeg, cinnamon, orange peel, and walnuts and stir to combine well. Set aside to cool.

Unroll the phyllo dough. (Keep the dough covered with a slightly damp lightweight dish towel.) Place the first sheet of phyllo on a work surface or baking sheet and brush with the clarified butter. Fold in half widthwise and brush again. Fold that half in half to make a 4-layer strip, 4½ × 14 inches. Place one-sixth of the filling at the bottom of the strip. Fold the dough strip like a flag, making a large triangle. Brush again with butter. Repeat with the rest of the filling. **It can be refrigerated several hours at this point.** Bake 10 to 15 minutes, or until golden brown. Serve hot.

Serves 6

CHRISTMAS COFFEE CAKE

It's such a pleasure to imagine one's loved ones eating homemade coffee cake on holiday mornings. This cake pleases grown-ups and children—as well as cooks, who find it easy to make and love being able to freeze it for several months.

1½ cups chopped pecans
½ cup packed light brown sugar
2 teaspoons ground cinnamon
½ cup grated coconut
Grated peel (no white attached) of 1 orange
4½ cups soft wheat all-purpose flour
2 teaspoons baking powder
2 teaspoons baking soda

½ teaspoon salt
1 cup (2 sticks) butter, at room temperature
1½ cups granulated sugar
2 teaspoons vanilla extract
1 teaspoon orange extract
4 eggs
2 cups sour cream

Preheat the oven to 350°F. Butter and flour a 10-inch tube pan and set aside.

In a small mixing bowl, combine the pecans, brown sugar, cinnamon, coconut, and orange peel. Set aside.

In a medium bowl, sift together the flour, baking powder, baking soda, and salt. In a mixer bowl, beat the butter until very soft. Gradually add the sugar and beat until light and fluffy. Beat in the vanilla and orange extracts. Beat in the eggs one at a time, beating well after each addition. On low speed, mix in the dry ingredients alternately with the sour cream, beginning and ending with the dry ingredients. Pour into the prepared pan. Sprinkle the topping onto the batter, pressing gently. Bake 50 to 60 minutes, or until a skewer inserted in the center comes out clean. Cool on a wire rack.

Serves 12 to 16

ABBY'S PECAN APPLECAKE

Talented cook Abby Mandel taught me this recipe many years ago—
only she used hazelnuts instead of pecans. This cake is perfect for a fall
picnic or tailgating, and because it's very rich a small slice is enough for most
people. It may be made in a large food processor as well as with a mixer. A
moist cake, it keeps well for days and freezes beautifully.

2 tablespoons butter, melted	2 large eggs
1½ cups sugar	⅓ cup milk
½ teaspoon ground cinnamon	2 tablespoons rum
½ teaspoon freshly grated nutmeg	2 teaspoons vanilla extract
1½ cups all-purpose flour	2 tablespoons finely chopped pecans
3 tart apples, such as Granny Smith,	1½ teaspoons baking powder
peeled, halved, and sliced (3 cups)	1½ teaspoons baking soda
½ cup (1 stick) butter	1½ teaspoons salt

Preheat the oven to 350°F.

Brush the sides of an 8 × 3¼-inch springform pan with the melted butter.
Mix together ½ cup sugar, cinnamon, nutmeg, and ¼ cup flour and sprinkle
the mixture evenly over the bottom of the pan. Wrap foil around the pan to
prevent leakage.

Starting at the outside edge, arrange a ring of apple slices in the pan, slightly overlapping and pointing to the center. (It will feel backwards.) Fill in the
center with another circle of apples, with some overlap occurring. Layer any
remaining apple slices evenly, overlapping to prevent the batter from escaping.

With a wooden spoon or electric mixer, beat together the butter and 1 cup
sugar. Add the eggs, milk, rum, and vanilla. The batter will look curdled. Add
1¼ cups flour, the nuts, baking powder, baking soda, and salt, beating only
until the flour is completely incorporated. Pour the batter over the apples and
spread evenly. Place the pan on a baking sheet and bake in the middle of the
oven until a toothpick inserted in the cake comes out clean, about 70 min-

utes. Cover with a piece of foil if the top begins to brown too quickly. Let the cake rest in the pan on a rack for 5 minutes, then, using a small, flexible knife, gently separate the sides of the cake from the pan. Invert the cake on the rack, letting it stay in the pan for another 10 minutes, then remove the pan, lifting it up carefully.

Serves 10 to 12

CRANBERRY CRISP

Tart and tangy, this dessert also has a crunchy topping. Omit the topping and you have a wonderful baked chutney for pork or poultry. This is good at room temperature or frozen and reheated.

5 Granny Smith apples, peeled, cored, and sliced into ½-inch wedges (about 3 cups)	*1 cup quick oats*
	½ cup packed brown sugar (light or dark)
2 cups fresh cranberries	*1 cup chopped pecans*
1 cup granulated sugar	*1 teaspoon vanilla extract*
2 tablespoons grated orange peel (no white attached)	*½ cup (1 stick) butter, melted*
1 tablespoon freshly grated or chopped ginger	

Preheat the oven to 325°F.

In a large bowl, toss together the apples, cranberries, and granulated sugar. Sprinkle with the orange peel and ginger and set aside. In another bowl, mix together the oats, brown sugar, and pecans. Spread the apple mixture in a buttered 9 × 13-inch baking dish. Press the oat mixture evenly on top. Mix together the vanilla and melted butter and pour over the entire surface. Bake 1 hour. Let sit 10 minutes before serving.

Serves 8

HEATH BAR CHEESECAKE

Cheesecakes are the easiest and fastest of the make-ahead desserts and this one is particularly so. Heath bars are one of my childhood weaknesses, and even today I am not immune to temptation. Now they are sold packaged in tiny bits—my undoing! This may be refrigerated several days or frozen.

1 5½-ounce package graham crackers
½ cup plus 2 tablespoons firmly packed
   dark brown sugar
8 tablespoons (1 stick) butter, melted

3 8-ounce packages cream cheese
4 large eggs
1 teaspoon vanilla extract
2 6-ounce packages Heath Bits

Preheat the oven to 350° F.

To make the crust, place the graham crackers, 2 tablespoons of brown sugar, and the melted butter in a food processor and process until fine crumbs are formed. If you don't have a processor, put the crackers in a plastic bag, crush them with a rolling pin, and then thoroughly combine with the brown sugar and melted butter. Press the crumbs into the bottom of a 9-inch greased springform pan. Place in the oven and bake 10 minutes, or until set. Remove from the oven and set aside.

In a large mixer bowl or in a food processor, beat the cream cheese until smooth and fluffy. Slowly add the remaining brown sugar and continue beating. Add the eggs and vanilla and beat until smooth. Add the Heath Bits and mix until just combined. Pour into the prepared pan, place it on a baking sheet, and put it in the middle rack of the preheated oven. Bake until set, about 50 to 60 minutes. Cool in the pan on a wire rack. Remove the sides. Refrigerate until thoroughly chilled.

Serves 8 to 10

LOW-CAL RICOTTA CHEESECAKE

When I was given this recipe, I was afraid I wouldn't like it, but I felt it was worth a try. To my delight, I found it very satisfying and was grateful for its lightness and low fat content. It's not usual to grease a pan for a graham cracker crust, but since the fat in the crust has been reduced, it's necessary. The pan of water helps keep the cake from cracking as it bakes.

1 5½-ounce package graham crackers

3 tablespoons butter

2 tablespoons packed dark brown sugar

1½ teaspoons ground ginger

2 15-ounce containers part-skim ricotta cheese

3 eggs

1 egg white

1 cup buttermilk

½ cup granulated sugar

1 tablespoon vanilla extract

Grated peel (no white attached) of 1 orange

2 tablespoons orange juice

Preheat the oven to 375°F. Grease a 9-inch springform pan or spray with nonstick spray.

To make the crust, place the graham crackers, butter, brown sugar, and ginger in the bowl of a food processor and process until well combined. Press into the bottom of the springform pan. Place the pan in the oven and bake 5 to 8 minutes. Remove from the oven and set aside to cool.

To make the filling, place the ricotta, eggs, egg white, buttermilk, sugar, vanilla, orange peel, and orange juice in the bowl of a food processor or electric mixer and process or mix until smooth. Pour the mixture into the cooled crust, put on a baking sheet, place in the oven, and place a pan of water in the bottom of the oven. Bake 45 to 60 minutes, or until set.

Serves 8 to 10

WHITE CHOCOLATE
CHEESECAKE

The title of this recipe says it all. This is a killer cheesecake—super rich— so be sure to have lots of folks to share the calories. To ensure the proper richness, use the best white chocolate available. The cheesecake must be made at least a day ahead and it freezes well.

**GRAHAM
CRACKER
CRUMBS**
One 5½-ounce package
of graham crackers will
make enough crumbs to
line a 9-inch springform
pan. Process them in a
food processor to fine
crumbs. You can also
crush them in a plastic
bag with a rolling pin.
In this case, you'll need
to crush only a few
at a time.

1 5½-ounce package graham crackers
3 tablespoons cocoa powder
2 tablespoons sugar
6 tablespoons (¾ stick) butter, melted
½ cup butter, softened
3 8-ounce packages cream cheese, at
   room temperature

¼ cup sugar
1 cup sour cream
1 pound good-quality white chocolate
   such as Lindt, melted and cooled
   slightly
4 large eggs
2 tablespoons vanilla extract

Preheat the oven to 350°F.

To make the crust, place the graham crackers, cocoa, sugar, and melted butter in a food processor and process until fine crumbs are formed. If you don't have a processor, put the crackers in a plastic bag, crush them with a rolling pin, and then thoroughly combine them with the cocoa, sugar, and melted butter. Press the crumbs into the bottom of a 10-inch springform pan. Bake 8 minutes, then remove from the oven and set aside to cool.

In a large mixer bowl or in a food processor, beat together the ½ cup butter and the cream cheese until smooth and fluffy. Continue to beat while slowly adding the sugar. Add the sour cream and beat until just combined. Add the melted white chocolate and beat. Add the eggs and vanilla and beat until smooth. Pour the mixture into the prepared pan, place it on a baking sheet, and put on the middle rack of the preheated oven. Bake until set, about 50 to 60 minutes. Cool in the pan on a wire rack, then remove the sides and refrigerate until thoroughly chilled.

Serves 10 to 12

MERINGUES

MAKE-AHEAD MERINGUES
Meringues and dacquoises should not be made the day you want to serve them. They do best made with no pressure of time, as they have their own minds and dry out according to the humidity of the day. They are best avoided in rainy, humid weather as is most sugar work.

This "Swiss" method ensures nice crisp meringues. Free of cholesterol (unless you choose to add a filling such as whipped cream or ice cream), they really are one of the easiest of all desserts to make.

When cooking meringues, remember you are really "drying" them, not baking them. Ideally, they are slightly more ivory than beige. Many people, however, prefer them a true beige, when they have a slightly caramel flavor. Knowing your oven is important. Many do not have an easily regulated low temperature. The first time you make them, keep checking and adjust the time according to your oven.

4 egg whites   ½ teaspoon vanilla extract
1 cup sugar

Preheat the oven to 250°F.

Place the egg whites in a bowl and whisk with a balloon whisk or electric whisk until they form very soft peaks.

Set the bowl over a pan of simmering water and whisk in the sugar. Add the vanilla. Continue whisking until the mixture forms a stiff peak, 5 minutes with an electric mixer, more by hand. They need only be beaten until they form a stiff peak and do not slide in the bowl. If beaten too long, they look rocky and start to separate. Remove from the heat and continue whisking until the meringue is cool.

Using a pastry bag and large star tube, pipe 3-inch rounds of meringue onto parchment paper, a nonstick baking sheet, or a greased and floured baking sheet. (You may also shape mounds with 2 tablespoons.) Bake until firm and ivory colored, 1 to 2 hours. If the meringues are to be filled with whipped cream, ice cream, or a favorite yogurt, turn them over when almost cooked, crack the center of the base to hollow the shell, and continue baking until dry.

Makes 14 to 16 large meringues

DACQUOISES

The key to this impressive dessert is long, slow cooking. Who would guess something so incredible would be so easy?

1 cup plus 3 tablespoons sugar
6 ounces ground blanched almonds or
   hazelnuts and almonds combined
1½ tablespoons cornstarch
6 egg whites
⅛ teaspoon salt
¼ teaspoon cream of tartar

Vanilla extract (a little over a teaspoon)
Scant ⅛ teaspoon almond extract

FILLING
1 pint strawberries
½ pint whipping cream, whipped stiffly
   with 3 tablespoons sugar

Preheat the oven to 250°F.

Grease and flour 2 baking sheets, then line with greased and floured wax paper or use parchment paper, which does not stick.

Make 3 8-inch circles on the sheets (or make 3 8-inch hearts if you prefer!). Place 1 cup sugar and the almonds in a bowl. Mix in the cornstarch. In another bowl, beat the egg whites until foamy. Add the salt and cream of tartar, then beat until stiff. Add the vanilla and almond extracts. Sprinkle the sugar-almond-cornstarch mixture on top of the egg whites. Fold in, then add the remaining 3 tablespoons sugar in thirds as each third is nearly blended. Do not overfold. Work quickly—don't take longer than a minute for the whole process. Fill a pastry bag with as much of the meringue as you can and pipe the meringue into the circle or heart shapes.

Place the pans in the upper middle and lower middle levels. Check after an hour and recheck every half hour. The dacquoises are done when they are lightly colored and when you can easily peel a corner of the paper off. When they're done, remove them carefully onto cake racks and cool. They will not seem totally "done," but they do crisp up as they cool. Be careful, because they crack and break . . . that is why they are difficult. If they crack, you can cover it up with whipped cream. I've seen cracked dacquoises pictured in gourmet magazines, so it is no tragedy.

To make the filling, slice half of the strawberries and mix with half of the cream. Sandwich the 3 rounds with the sliced strawberries and cream. Coat the top and sides with the rest of the cream and garnish with the remaining strawberries.

Serves 6 to 8

RASPBERRY MERINGUE CAKE

The crisp meringue layer, topped with cream and layered with sherbet, is a stunning addition to any meal. Meringue rounds are "dried" rather than baked in a slow oven. They may be frozen and the whole decorated cake may be frozen for up to a month.

8 egg whites
2 cups sugar

1 quart raspberry sherbet, softened in the
refrigerator for 30 minutes
2 cups whipping cream

Preheat the oven to 200°F.

Beat the egg whites to a stiff peak. Fold in the sugar. Line 3 pans with parchment paper and draw three 8-inch circles. Place the egg whites in a piping bag and pipe 3 layers in equal rounds or spread in 3 rounds with a spatula. Bake for 2 to 3 hours.

Layer the meringue and sherbet, beginning and ending with the meringue rounds. Spread the whipped cream over the top and sides of the cake and pipe rosettes on top and around the base. Store in the freezer until 15 minutes before serving.

Serves 8 to 10

CHOCO-MINT BOULE DE NEIGE

This simple adaptation of the French "Ball of Snow" is remarkably easy for the applause it is guaranteed to receive. The chocolate mint morsels lend a subtle flavor, mimicking high-quality imported chocolate without the investment. This is one of our all-time favorite desserts.

It takes very little time to assemble and bakes unattended. I usually double the recipe so that I have a spare snowball for emergencies. Wrapped in foil in the freezer, it will be safe from the marauders! It will keep in the refrigerator up to 2 weeks and it freezes for 3 months.

1 10-ounce package chocolate mint morsels	TOPPING
	1 cup heavy (whipping) cream
½ cup water	2 tablespoons sugar
1 cup sugar	1 teaspoon vanilla extract
1 cup (2 sticks) butter, at room temperature	
4 eggs	GARNISH
1 tablespoon vanilla extract	Chocolate shards or leaves (page 187)
½ teaspoon peppermint extract (optional)	(optional)

Preheat the oven to 350°F. Line a 5-cup ovenproof bowl with a double thickness of foil. Melt the chocolate with the water and sugar over low heat or in the microwave; cool slightly. Transfer the chocolate mixture to a mixing bowl or food processor and beat in the butter. Add the eggs one by one, followed by the vanilla and peppermint extract if using, beating after each addition.

Pour the mixture into the foil-lined mold; bake 1 hour, or until a thick crust has formed on top. Remove from the oven and cool. It will collapse—don't worry. Cover tightly and refrigerate until solid, 2 to 3 hours or overnight. *This can be done several days in advance.*

For the topping, combine the cream, sugar, and vanilla and whip until stiff. Place the cream in a piping bag with a star tip. Remove the snowball from the

WHIPPED CREAM
For better results when piping or decorating, whip cream in the food processor. Use the steel knife, add the heavy cream, sugar, and flavoring, and process about 30 seconds, checking frequently to avoid overprocessing. The food processor does not produce as much volume as beating by hand or with a mixer, bu the cream pipes and decorates more easily and does not weep as readily. To avoid weeping, spoon the whipped cream into a piece of cheesecloth or in a fine sieve and let drain a few hours before using. To store a cream-decorated dessert, cover it with a large glass or plastic cake cover and place it in a larger, airtight container (like a Tupperware box or cake storer). Alternatively, you can poke long skewers into the cream and lightly wrap the whole thing with plastic wrap; it looks like a crazy beehive, but it works.

bowl and peel off the foil. Place, flat-side down, on a serving dish. Pipe rosettes of whipped cream over the entire surface until no chocolate shows. Chill until served. Garnish with chocolate leaves if desired.

Serves 6 to 8

TIP : Use a plastic bag with one corner cut off as a piping bag.

CHOCOLATE SHARDS

This quick delight is perfect after a heavy or filling meal when just a taste of sweetness is needed to cap off your dinner. The subtle taste of mint makes the chocolate seem more expensive than it really is. This should be made several hours or several days ahead.

1 (10-ounce) package chocolate mint morsels

In a saucepan or in a measuring cup in the microwave, melt the chocolate over low heat, stirring so the chocolate will not scorch. Let cool for 5 minutes and then spread the chocolate on parchment, waxed paper, or aluminum foil about ⅛-inch thick. Allow to harden, then break into irregular pieces and serve alone in a pretty silver bowl or use as a garnish for Choco-Mint Boule de Neige, ice cream, custards, or fresh berries. If you want to make chocolate leaves, wash and thoroughly dry several rose or mint leaves. With a small brush, "paint" the chocolate on the underside of the leaf. Allow to harden and gently remove the leaf from the chocolate.

Serves 6 to 8

ITALIAN BISCOTTI

These crunchy cookies are perfect for making ahead and keeping airtight or frozen. They lend their grace to large buffets and are great for snacks or as an accompaniment to ice cream.

1 cup sugar
3 eggs
¼ cup (½ stick) butter, melted
1 teaspoon fennel or anise seeds, lightly
    crushed

1 teaspoon orange extract
2 cups all-purpose flour, sifted
2 teaspoons baking powder
¾ cup whole unblanched almonds

Preheat the oven to 350°F.

In a medium mixing bowl, beat the sugar and eggs together until creamy. Beat in the melted butter, fennel seeds, and orange extract. Mix together the flour and baking powder, add to the batter, and beat until well blended. Stir in the nuts. Place the dough in the refrigerator and chill for at least 1 hour. *The chilled dough can be kept refrigerated for up to 3 days.*

Shape the dough into a 6 × 9-inch oval 1½ inches thick and place on an ungreased baking sheet. Bake for 20 to 25 minutes, or until firm and lightly browned. Remove the pan from the oven and cool slightly. Transfer the dough to a cutting board and slice diagonally into ½-inch thick pieces. Arrange, cut-side down, on the baking sheet and return to the oven. Bake an additional 15 minutes. Transfer the baked biscotti to wire racks to cool.

Makes 18

GRANDMOTHER KREISER'S ICEBOX COOKIES

STORING COOKIES
Always store cookies of different types separately, as they exchange moisture and flavors. Sturdy cookies can be kept in the freezer in a plastic bag. Fragile ones should be layered in a structured container and separated by wax paper if necessary.

The Kreiser women were renowned bakers. Indomitable, busy women, they liked to be able to make the best use of their time. What better way than having a dough ready to be sliced and baked at will?

The look of these crisp cookies is deceiving. You might be fooled into thinking they were peanut butter cookies, but their flavor is redolent of spices. The thinner they are sliced the better.

2 cups (4 sticks) margarine (not butter)
1 cup firmly packed light brown sugar
1 cup granulated sugar
2 eggs
2 teaspoons fresh lemon juice
2 teaspoons vanilla extract
4½ cups all-purpose flour

¼ teaspoon baking powder
¼ teaspoon baking soda
½ teaspoon cardamom
¼ cup chopped walnuts, pecans, or
 almonds
½ teaspoon salt
1 teaspoon ground cinnamon

Beat together the margarine and sugars until fluffy. Add the eggs and beat until well combined. Beat in the lemon juice and vanilla. Mix together the flour, baking powder, baking soda, cardamom, nuts, salt, and cinnamon, then stir the dry ingredients into the margarine mixture to make a stiff dough. Shape the dough into a long cylinder and refrigerate overnight. **The dough can be frozen at this point.**

Preheat the oven to 375°F.

Slice the cookie dough paper thin—⅛ inch is best—and arrange on a baking sheet.

Bake the cookies until light brown, about 13 to 15 minutes.

Makes 36

SUMMER PUDDING

Who, I wonder, originally thought of this marvelous dish? I remember first tasting it many years ago at an English lawn party. But my friend Virginia made it just recently for a block party while I visited her in England. It was the hit of the party, and, as she mentioned to me behind her hand, it's so ridiculously easy! It is best made a day or two ahead and it freezes, too.

7 cups mixed berries (raspberries, straw-
    berries, blueberries, loganberries, or the
    like)

1 cup sugar
10 to 15 slices firm-textured white
    bread, crusts removed

Place 6 cups of the berries in a saucepan with the sugar. Reserve the remaining cup for garnish. Bring to the boil, reduce the heat, and simmer slowly until the fruit has released its juices, about 10 minutes. This should equal 3 cups. Set aside to cool slightly.

Butter a 1½-quart soufflé dish. Line the dish tightly with the bread slices, cutting to fit as necessary. Do not overlap the bread slices—it should appear like a seamless cloth. Pour the cooked berries into the bread-lined dish. (The berries will only fill three-quarters of the bowl.) Top the berries with additional bread slices, covering them completely. Place plastic wrap on top of the bread. Place a slightly smaller plate directly on top of the plastic wrap in the dish. Put a 2- to 3-pound weight (such as a can) on the plate. Refrigerate overnight. *This can be done up to 3 days in advance.*

To serve, remove the weight and plate and run a knife around the edges of the pudding to loosen. Invert the pudding onto a serving plate. Top with the remaining berries. Pour any remaining juices over the pudding until every bit of bread is stained.

Serves 4 to 6

ORANGES WITH GINGER CUSTARD

This is a decadently rich custard subtly flavored with ginger. It is great served over the oranges as we have done here but is also good piped into an eclair or cream puff. To heighten the ginger flavor, 1 to 2 tablespoons of finely chopped candied ginger can be sprinkled over the custard.

1 cup milk
1½ cups whipping cream
10 egg yolks
½ cup sugar

3 tablespoons finely chopped fresh ginger
2 teaspoons vanilla extract
4 to 6 navel oranges

In a large mixing bowl, lightly whisk together the milk, cream, egg yolks, sugar, and ginger. Place the mixture in a large heavy saucepan and cook over medium heat, stirring constantly, until it has thickened and coats the back of a spoon. The mixture should reach a temperature of 170°F. Strain the mixture to remove any small pieces of cooked egg. Stir in the vanilla. Refrigerate at least 2 hours. *The custard can be refrigerated for up to 2 days.*

To serve, use a sharp knife to cut the peel and pith off of the oranges. Slice the peeled oranges crosswise and arrange on individual dessert plates. Top each serving with some custard.

Serves 4 to 6

GINGER–APRICOT FLAN

This delicate caramel and apricot-ginger custard cools and refreshes as it slides down your throat. It's best made a full day ahead to give it that silky smoothness and to chill it properly, and it will keep for 2 days. The only tricky part of this recipe is making the caramel, but sugar is cheap, and mistakes easily rectified. After that step, all that remains is the long, slow cooking in the oven. While you are waiting for it to be done, you can be making stews on top of the stove.

CANDIED GINGER
Candied ginger may be found in the spice section of the grocery store or in Oriental grocery stores in boxes, where it is much less expensive than in the small jars found in regular grocery stores.

1 cup canned apricot halves (1 17-ounce can)
1½ cups sugar
1 tablespoon corn syrup
⅓ cup water
2⅔ cups milk

Peel of 1 lemon (peel off strips with a vegetable peeler)
3 whole eggs
5 egg yolks
2½ teaspoons vanilla extract
¼ cup chopped candied ginger

Preheat the oven to 325°F.

Drain the apricot halves and puree in a food processor or blender until smooth. Set aside.

Dissolve 1 cup sugar with the corn syrup and water in a heavy pan over low heat without boiling. When dissolved, brush the insides of the pan with a wet pastry brush to remove the sugar crystals. Turn up the heat, bring to the boil, and boil until the liquid turns a golden caramel color, about 10 minutes.

Meanwhile, warm a 1-quart ovenproof soufflé dish in the oven. Using oven mitts, remove the dish from the oven, pour in the hot caramel, and tilt the dish from side to side to coat the bottom and lower sides with the caramel. (Any extra caramel can be drizzled in shapes on parchment paper or an oiled marble slab for garnishes; remove when hardened and keep in an airtight container or the freezer until ready to use.) Add the milk to the original caramel pan with the lemon peel and heat until small bubbles form around the side.

In a large mixing bowl, combine the eggs, egg yolks, and the remaining ½ cup sugar. Pour the hot milk into the egg mixture all at once, stirring constantly. Strain the mixture into another bowl and stir in the vanilla, the apricot puree, and the candied ginger. Pour the custard carefully into the prepared soufflé dish; it will foam if not poured slowly.

Place a kitchen towel on the bottom of a roasting pan with sides. This will help insulate the flan and prevent bubbles on the bottom of the dish. Put the soufflé dish on the towel in the middle of the pan. Carefully pour enough boiling water into the pan to come halfway up the sides of the soufflé dish. Place the roasting pan in the center of the oven and cook approximately 1¾ to 2 hours, or until the custard is set and a knife inserted in the center comes out clean. Do not let the water boil, as the boiling will overcook the custard and make holes in it; if necessary, add cold water to the pan. Remove the pan from the oven; remove the soufflé dish from the pan. Cool slightly, then cover and refrigerate at least 3 hours.

When the flan has chilled completely, run a knife around the edge, then shake the dish or pull the custard lightly away from the sides with a knife. Place a shallow serving plate on top, then invert the dish to unmold the flan. The caramel forms a topping and sauce. Serve chilled. Garnish with caramel squiggles if desired.

Serves 8 to 10

INDESTRUCTIBLE BAKED
LEMON SOUFFLE PUDDING

This old-time soufflé pudding is delicious. It's a soufflélike cake on top of a soft, hidden custardy pudding. I like it because I can have it assembled up to several hours ahead and pop it in the oven just before sitting down for my main course, so its glorious fragrance fills the air as we eat. When preparing it, the butter will solidify and not incorporate properly if the milk is very cold, so be sure the milk is lukewarm. Don't be surprised if the pudding looks curdled at the end. Just serve it any way it comes out—you'll love it. It can be reheated in the microwave or oven or served cold. Also, I've caught many a person standing in front of the refrigerator eating from a half-empty lemon pudding dish until it was all gone.

6 tablespoons butter, softened	*2 tablespoons all-purpose flour*
2 teaspoons grated lemon peel (no white	*4 tablespoons fresh lemon juice, strained*
attached)	*2 cups warm whole milk*
¼ cup granulated sugar	*5 egg whites*
5 egg yolks	*½ cup confectioners' sugar (optional)*

Preheat the oven to 350° F. Butter an 8-inch casserole or soufflé dish.

In a mixing bowl, beat together the butter and the lemon peel. Gradually add the sugar, beating until the mixture is light. Stir in the egg yolks, flour, and lemon juice. Add the milk, stirring, a little at a time. In a separate bowl, beat the egg whites until stiff. Gently fold the whites into the batter. Pour into a buttered dish. ***The pudding can be made several hours ahead to this point***.

Place the soufflé dish in a pan filled with enough hot water to come halfway up the side of the dish and bake 35 to 40 minutes. Serve immediately, sprinkled with confectioners' sugar if desired.

Serves 4 to 6

MARBLED CHOCOLATE MOUSSE

Everyone always tells me people want low-calorie desserts, but I'm tempted to disbelieve them. For instance, when I hosted a committee lunch recently, I devised a low-cal treat. I also had this Marbled Chocolate Mousse on hand in the freezer. I served both. No one touched the low-cal one—all chose this mousse! In case you didn't notice, it's loaded with calories. If you like, the chocolate mixture can be swirled together in six separate bowls or goblets, creating spectacular individual dessert servings. Sprinkle with the shaved chocolate before serving.

DARK MOUSSE
8 ounces dark or semisweet chocolate
¼ cup heavy cream
1 teaspoon rum or vanilla extract
2 tablespoons butter
4 eggs, separated

WHITE MOUSSE
4 ounces white chocolate
2 tablespoons cream
½ teaspoon vanilla extract
1 tablespoon butter
2 eggs, separated

GARNISH
2 ounces white or dark chocolate, shaved

The dark and white mousses are made separately, but the method is the same. Melt the chocolate, cream, rum or vanilla, and butter in a heavy pan over low heat. Off the heat, add the egg yolks one at a time, stirring well after each addition. In a clean bowl, beat the egg whites until soft peaks form. Stir a little of the beaten whites into the chocolate mixture to lighten it, then gently fold the chocolate into the egg whites. Repeat this procedure for the second mousse.

In a 1½-quart glass bowl, ladle half of the dark mousse, cover with all of the white mousse, then top with the remaining dark mousse. With a knife or spatula gently swirl the 2 mixtures together to create a marbled effect. Refrigerate for at least 6 hours. Serve sprinkled with white or dark chocolate shavings if desired.

Serves 6 to 8

GRAPE AND APRICOT TART

Once my friend and co-worker Ray was looking for a perfect picnic tart. As a caterer, he's always judged by how beautiful his food is—and he always wants new ideas. This one was a real keeper; every time I saw fresh apricots in the store that year, I made it again; it was that good.

The brown butter crust adds a new dimension to the fresh fruit and almond paste.

1 11-inch Browned Butter Tart Pastry
  shell (page 200)
Confectioners' sugar
1 7-ounce package marzipan, at room
  temperature

4 apricots, halved, pitted, and cut into
  wedges
1 cup green seedless grapes, halved
½ cup red seedless grapes, halved
1 tablespoon granulated sugar

Preheat the oven to 400°F.

Line an 11-inch tart pan with Browned Butter Tart Pastry. On a board dusted with confectioners' sugar, roll the marzipan into a 10-inch circle and place it in the unbaked shell. Arrange the apricot wedges in a concentric circle around the outer edge of the pastry. In the center of the pie shell, mound the green and red grapes. Sprinkle with the sugar. Place the tart on a baking sheet and bake about 45 minutes. Remove from the oven and let cool completely before removing from the pan. Cut into wedges and serve.

Serves 8 to 10

AMETHYST PIE

This pie with its gorgeous purple color has a fantastic flavor that combines the tartness of cranberries with the sweetness of blueberries. You can use frozen blueberries if fresh are unavailable; just be sure to drain any excess liquid. If you have a Southern "sweet tooth" as I do, you may want to increase the sugar or substitute 1 cup additional blueberries, decreasing the tart cranberries. Adapt this recipe to suit your family's personal taste.

2 cups fresh or frozen blueberries

2 cups fresh or frozen cranberries

1½ cups plus 1 tablespoon sugar

¾ cup cornstarch

2 tablespoons grated orange peel (no
  white attached)

2 tablespoons orange juice

2 teaspoons vanilla extract

Pastry for 1 9-inch double-crust pie
  (page 201)

1 cup slivered almonds

2 tablespoons butter

1 tablespoon milk

GARNISH

1 cup whipped cream

Preheat the oven to 375°F.

In a large bowl, combine the blueberries, cranberries, 1½ cups of sugar, cornstarch, orange peel, orange juice, and vanilla. Pour the fruit mixture into an unbaked 9-inch piecrust, sprinkle with the slivered almonds, and dot with butter. Top the fruit with the top crust and crimp the edges to seal. Make 4 or 5 decorative cutouts or slits in the top of the crust to allow steam to escape. Brush the top of the pie with the milk and then sprinkle evenly with 1 tablespoon of sugar. Place the pie on a baking sheet and bake for 1 hour, or until the filling is hot and bubbly. Cover the pie with foil if the edges begin to brown too quickly. Cool completely on a wire rack before serving. Serve with whipped cream if desired.

Serves 6 to 8

MARKHAM FAMILY LEMON
MERINGUE PIE

John Markham, a friend who was the book rep for Random House when
I wrote *New Southern Cooking*, loves good food and entertains frequently. He often uses old family recipes and he shared this one from his great-
grandmother with me.

7 eggs, separated
⅔ cup plus 3 tablespoons sugar
Grated peel (no white attached) and juice
   of 2 lemons

1 9-inch piecrust, prebaked (page 201)

Preheat the oven to 350°F.

In a heatproof mixing bowl, beat the egg yolks with ⅔ cup sugar until pale
in color, smooth, thick, and creamy, about 5 to 7 minutes. Add the lemon peel
and juice, beating constantly. Set the bowl over a saucepan of simmering water
and cook over medium heat, stirring constantly, until the mixture thickens,
about 10 minutes. Remove from the heat. In a separate bowl, beat 3 of the
egg whites to stiff peaks. Stir one-quarter of the whites into the lemon mixture and then fold this mixture into the beaten whites. Pour the lemon custard
into the baked piecrust. Beat the remaining 4 egg whites with the remaining
3 tablespoons sugar to stiff peaks. Spread the meringue over the pie, being
careful to spread it to the edges on all sides so the meringue will not shrink.
Bake the pie about 10 minutes, or until the top of the meringue is browned.
Cool before slicing.

The custard can also be used as a topping for pound cake or to fill small
tartlets, topped with fresh berries.

Serves 6 to 8

PLUM PIE

There comes a point each summer when the plums are just perfect—in my area it's August. When that moment arrives, by all means try this delicious confection. It works with both red and black plums, and the butter and sugar topping gives it an unusual crispness and sparkle. Do not peel the plums or you will lose that tart and tangy flavor the skin imparts.

Pastry for 1 9-inch double-crust pie
   (page 201)
6 cups sliced plums
1 cup plus 1 tablespoon sugar
¼ cup all-purpose flour

¼ cup cornstarch
½ teaspoon ground cinnamon
2 teaspoons chopped candied ginger
2 tablespoons butter, softened

Preheat the oven to 425° F. Divide the piecrust in half and roll one to line a 9-inch pie pan. Roll out the second half into an 11-inch round for the top and keep chilled.

In a large bowl, mix together the sliced plums, 1 cup sugar, the flour, cornstarch, cinnamon, and ginger. Pour the fruit mixture into the piecrust. Top with the second crust and crimp the edges to seal. Make 4 or 5 slits or decorative cutouts in the top of the pie to allow steam to escape. Dot the crust with the softened butter and sprinkle with the remaining 1 tablespoon sugar. Place the pie on a cookie sheet to catch any drips and bake for 15 minutes. Reduce the heat to 375° F. and bake for 50 to 60 minutes longer, until the filling is hot and bubbly and the top crust is golden brown. If the top begins to brown too quickly, cover loosely with foil, removing it for the last 5 minutes of baking. Cool on a wire rack and serve warm.

Serves 6 to 8

BROWNED BUTTER
TART PASTRY

I 'd never had a browned butter tart until Ray brought me this recipe, which I love. By browning the butter, you get a wonderfully nutty, rich pastry. Be aware that you will lose about one-third of the original butter by volume. Be sure not to use any of the brown sediment on the bottom of the pan; you want only the pure browned butterfat.

1 cup (2 sticks) butter
1½ cups all-purpose flour

½ teaspoon salt
6 to 8 tablespoons ice water

In a small saucepan, melt the butter and cook over low heat until the butter browns, about 3 to 4 minutes. Pour into a glass measuring cup and refrigerate until firm, about 4 hours.

In a food processor or large bowl, mix together the flour and salt. Add the chilled butter and cut in until the pieces are about the size of peas. Add the ice water a tablespoon at a time and mix just until the dough begins to hold together. Flour your board and flatten the dough ball into a round disk. Wrap in plastic wrap and refrigerate 1 hour. Remove from the refrigerator and roll the dough into a 12-inch circle on a floured board. Line an 11-inch tart pan with the dough, gently pressing the dough into place without stretching it. Fill and bake as desired.

Serves 8 to 10

PERFECT PIECRUST

**STORE-
BOUGHT
PIECRUST**
Store-bought frozen
piecrust can be used
for this tart. Buy 2
frozen crusts and
defrost until pliable.
Move one to the 9-inch
pie plate. Fill the pie
as directed. Flour a
board and roll out the
second crust lightly to
smooth. Place on top
as directed.

This is the perfect piecrust for a beginner. The secret to a flaky crust is to use well-chilled shortening and ice-cold water. This helps to retard the gluten or protein from developing and makes rolling out the dough much easier. It can be frozen in a ball for up to 2 months or already rolled out and prebaked for a month.

1½ cups all-purpose flour   *10 tablespoons shortening, well chilled*
¾ teaspoon salt   *4 to 6 tablespoons ice water*

Mix the flour and salt together in a bowl. Cut in the shortening with a pastry blender or fork until the mixture resembles cornmeal. Add the ice water a little at a time, tossing the mixture with the pastry blender or fork until it is moist and holds together. Gather into a ball and flatten. Cover and let rest a few minutes. **The dough can be tightly wrapped and frozen for up to 2 months.**

Flour a board or wax paper, and, using a floured or stockinged rolling pin, roll the pastry out ⅛ inch thick or less and at least 1½ to 2 inches larger than your pan. Fold in quarters. Place the pastry in a 9-inch pie pan and unfold. Trim the pastry 1 inch larger than the pie pan and decorate by folding the overhanging pastry under itself, then either pressing the tines of a fork around the edge to form a pattern or fluting, using your 2 thumbs to pinch the dough all around the edge so that the dough stands up where it has been pinched. Place in the freezer or chill in the refrigerator for 30 minutes before baking.

To prebake the piecrust, preheat the oven to 425°F. Crumple a piece of wax paper, then spread it out to the edges of the pan. To make a weight, fill the paper with raw rice or dried peas. Bake 20 minutes. Carefully remove the paper and rice or peas. (The rice or peas may be used again the next time you prebake a piecrust.) **The baked shell can be frozen for a month or so.** Fill the crust with a filling and bake according to filling directions. If the filling requires no cooking, bake the pie shell 10 minutes more.

Serves 6 to 8

ALL-FRUIT COBBLER

My cobblers are not made with piecrusts but with batters that puff up and brown around the fruit. Once combined, cobblers bake happily unattended while dinner is being served, but they can also be made ahead and frozen. If using sweetened frozen fruit, decrease the quantity of sugar.

1 cup sugar
2 cups blueberries, raspberries, or sliced
* strawberries or peaches*
½ cup (1 stick) butter

1 cup all-purpose flour
1½ teaspoons baking powder
½ teaspoon salt
1 cup milk

Preheat the oven to 375° F.

In a mixing bowl, toss the sugar together with the fruit. Put the butter in an 8 × 11-inch ovenproof serving dish and place in the oven to melt. Sift the flour, baking powder, and salt together into a bowl. Stir in the milk to make a batter. Pull the hot dish of melted butter out of the oven and pour in the batter, which will bubble around the sides. Quickly spoon the fruit and its juices evenly over the batter. Return to the oven and bake until the dough is brown and has risen up around the fruit, about 30 to 40 minutes.

Serves 6 to 8

BIBLIOGRAPHY

Amezúa, Clara; Arenillas, Ángeles; and Capel, José Carlos. *From Spain with Olive Oil*. Madrid: Asoliva, 1988.

Barron, Rosemary. *Flavors of Greece*. New York: William Morrow and Co, Inc., 1991.

Behan, Eileen. *Eat Well, Lose Weight While Breastfeeding*. New York: Villard Books, 1992.

Brody, Jane. *Good Food Gourmet*. New York: Bantam Books, 1990.

Carluccio, Antonio. *A Taste of Italy*. New York: Little, Brown, 1986.

Carrier, Robert. *A Taste of Morocco*. New York: Clarkson N. Potter, Inc., 1987.

Dragonwagon, Crescent. *Dairy Hollow House Soup and Bread*. New York: Workman Press, 1992.

Dupree, Nathalie. *Nathalie Dupree's Matters of Taste*. New York: Alfred A. Knopf, 1990.

————. *New Southern Cooking*. New York: Alfred A. Knopf, 1987.

Elliot, Ross. *The Complete Vegetarian Cuisine*. New York: Pantheon Books.

Food & Wine, 1992.

Goldstein, Joyce. *The Mediterranean Kitchen*. New York: William Morrow and Co., Inc., 1989.

Good Housekeeping Illustrated Book of Desserts. New York: Hearst Books, 1989.

Gourmet, August 1976.

Green, Jane and Choate, Judith. *The Gift Givers' Cookbook*. New York: Simon and Schuster, 1971.

Hadamuscin, John. *The Holidays*. New York: Harmony Books, 1986.

Hadda, Geri. *Coffee Cakes*. New York: Simon and Schuster, 1992.

Hazan, Marcella. *Essentials of Classic Italian Cooking*. New York: Alfred A. Knopf, 1992.

Hazelton, Nika. *The Regional Italian Kitchen*. New York: M. Evans and Co., Inc., 1978.

Kurzweil, Raymond. *The 10% Solution for a Healthy Life*. New York: Crown Publishers, Inc., 1993.

Langseth-Christensen, Lillian. *Gourmet's Old Vienna Cookbook*. New York: Gourmet Books, Inc., 1982.

McGee, Harold. *On Food and Cooking*. New York: Macmillan Publishing, 1984.

Netzer, Corrine T. *101 Low Calorie Recipes*. New York: Dell Publishing, 1993.

Olney, Judith. *Judith Olney on Bread*. New York: Crown Publishers, Inc., 1985.

O'Neill, Molly. *New York Cook Book*. New York: Workman Press, 1992.

Prestcott, W. Peter. *"A Rich and Rustic Italian Dish," Food & Wine*.

Recipe Club of Saint Paul's Greek Orthodox Cathedral, The. *The Complete Book of Greek Cooking*. New York: Harper & Row, 1990.

Safdie, Edward J. *New Spa Food*. New York: Clarkson N. Potter, Inc., 1990.

Sahni, Julie. *Classical Indian Cooking*. New York: William Morrow and Co., Inc., 1980.

Shaw, Diana. *Sweet Basil, Garlic, Tomatoes and Chives*. New York: Harmony Books, 1992.

Willan, Anne. *La Varenne Pratique*. New York: Crown Publishers, Inc., 1989.

Wolfert, Paula. *The Sharing Table. A Book of Eastern Mediterranean Food*. New York: HarperCollins, 1993.

Yan, Martin. *The Chinese Chef*. Garden City, NY: Doubleday and Co., Inc., 1985.

INDEX

EQUIVALENT IMPERIAL AND METRIC MEASUREMENTS

American cooks use standard containers, the 8-ounce cup and a tablespoon that takes exactly 16 level fillings to fill that cup level. Measuring by cup makes it very difficult to give weight equivalents, as a cup of densely packed butter will weigh considerably more than a cup of flour. The easiest way therefore to deal with cup measurements in recipes is to take the amount by volume rather than by weight. Thus the equation reads:

1 cup = 240 ml = 8 fl. oz.   ½ cup = 120 ml = 4 fl. oz.

It is possible to buy a set of American cup measures in major stores around the world.

In the States, butter is often measured in sticks. One stick is the equivalent of 8 tablespoons. One tablespoon of butter is therefore the equivalent to 1/2 ounce/15 grams.

Liquid Measures

Fluid ounces	U.S.	Imperial	Milliliters
	1 teaspoon	1 teaspoon	5
1/4	2 teaspoons	1 dessert spoon	7
½	1 tablespoon	1 tablespoon	15
1	2 tablespoon	2 tablespoon	28
2	¼ cup	4 tablespoon	56
4	½ cup or ¼ pint		110
5		¼ pint or 1 gill	140
6	¾ cup		170
8	1 cup or ½ pint		225
9			250, ¼ liter
10	1¼ cups	½ pint	280
12	1½ cups	¾ pint	340
15	¾ pint		420
16	2 cups or 1 pint		450
18	2¼ cups		500, ½ liter
20	2½ cups	1 pint	560
24	3 cups		675
			or 1½ pints
25		1¼ pints	700
27	3½ cups		750
30	3¾ cups	1½ pints	840
32	4 cups or 2 pints		900
	or 1 quart		
35		1¾ pints	980
36	4½ cups		1000, 1 liter
40	5 cups	2 pints or 1 quart	1120
	or 2½ pints		
48	6 cups or 3 pints		1350
50		2½ pints	1400
60	7½ cups	3 pints	1680
64	8 cups or 4 pints		1800
	or 2 quarts		
72	9 cups		2000, 2 liters

Solid Measures

U.S. and Imperial Measures		Metric Measures	
ounces	pounds	grams	kilos
1		28	
2		56	
3 ½		100	
4	¼	112	
5		140	
6		168	
8	½	225	
9		250	¼
12	¾	340	
16	1	450	
18		500	½
20	1¼	560	
24	1½	675	
27		750	¾
28	1¾	780	
32	2	900	
36	2¼	1000	1
40	2½	1100	
48	3	1350	
54		1500	1½
64	4	1800	
72	4½	2000	2
80	5	2250	2¼
90		2500	2½
100	6	2800	2¾

Oven Temperature Equivalents

Fahrenheit	Celsius	Gas Mark	Description
225	110	¼	Cool
250	130	½	
275	140	1	Very Slow
300	150	2	
325	170	3	Slow
350	180	4	Moderate
375	190	5	
400	200	6	Moderately Hot
425	220	7	Fairly Hot
450	230	8	Hot
475	240	9	Very Hot
500	250	10	Extremely Hot

Linear and Area Measures

1 inch	2.54 centimeters
1 foot	0.3048 meters
1 square inch	6.4516 square centimeters
1 square foot	929.03 square centimeters

Printed in the United States
by Baker & Taylor Publisher Services